A Treasury of
Carolina Tales

A Treasury of Carolina Tales

Webb Garrison

RUTLEDGE HILL PRESS
Nashville, Tennessee

Published in Nashville, Tennessee, by Rutledge Hill Press, Inc., 211 Seventh Avenue North, Nashville, Tennessee 37219

Typography by D&T/Bailey Typesetting, Inc., Nashville, Tennessee

Library of Congress Cataloging-in-Publication Data

Garrison, Webb B.
  A treasury of Carolina tales / Webb Garrison.
    p. cm.
  Includes index.
  ISBN 1-55853-449-0 (paperback)
  1. North Carolina—History, Local. 2. South Carolina—History,
Local 3. Legends—North Carolina. 4. Legends—South Carolina.
I. Title.
F254.5.G37 1988
975.6—dc19   88-3188
                                                             CIP

Printed in the United States of America
6 7 8 9 — 99 98 97 96

Two Carolinas Were First One

When Queen Elizabeth I, called "the virgin queen" by her courtiers, sent Walter Raleigh to explore the New World, she granted him "unknown lands" north of Florida. In return, Raleigh named the territory he explored Virginia in honor of the queen's chastity.

In 1629 King Charles I split Virginia in two, granting land from Albemarle Sound southward to Florida to Sir Robert Heath. In theory Heath's "empire," which he called Carolina from the Latin form of his ruler's name, stretched from the Atlantic Ocean to the South Seas. Charles asked very little of Heath. He simply was required to keep a gold crown on hand in case Charles should visit, which he never did.

Charles's son, Charles II, gave Carolina to eight of his lords in 1663. As depicted in A. H. Jaillot's 1696 map, published in Amsterdam, the colony was clearly too big for efficient management. Hence holdings were split into North Carolina and South Carolina in 1711. The division has continued since then.

The tales in this volume focus on people, places, and events of both Carolinas. Some emphasize North Carolina, others South Carolina, yet others both. In view of the states' common heritage, it is fitting that these tales of action and adventure be presented in one volume.

Here's hoping that you enjoy these stories. You may even receive a few surprises!

—Webb Garrison

Table of Contents

Part Six: They Left Their Mark

A Treasury of
Carolina Tales

PART ONE:

They Don't Make Them Like That Anymore

Dr. John Romulus ("Goat-gland") Brinkley. [INTERNATIONAL NEWS SERVICE]

1

Jackson County M.D. Pioneered in Organ Transplants

"I've got the mountains and their waterfalls in my blood," listeners to radio station XER were told often and earnestly. John Romulus Brinkley, M.D., had built the station just across the Mexican border from Del Rio, Texas, far from his native Jackson County, North Carolina.

Gesturing gracefully with his diamond-heavy hands, Brinkley used radio to enrich himself. "My dear, dear friends," he often began, "I thank you for your love—and for your letters. I promise to answer each and every letter, soon. But, oh my friends, you must help me. Remember that I must pay office rent, hire stenographers, and buy postage stamps.

"Only when you send my small fee of two dollars along with your questions will it be possible for me to share my medical knowledge with you."

No one knows how many listeners wrote regularly, faithfully enclosing Brinkley's fee. But the wattage of XER was boosted several times, until it became the most powerful radio station in the world. John Brinkley had come a long, long way from his Smoky Mountains boyhood.

Yet that powerful radio station and its hosts of listeners constituted only a sideline—and a small one at that—for the physician. Decades before surgeons made world news by transplanting a baboon's heart into a dying child, Brinkley was specializing in transplanting testicles from goats to men.

Tourists and visitors liked to pose for photos at hospital entrance.

John Brinkley's career may well have been launched by his unique middle name, Romulus, the same as the founder of ancient Rome who was saved from starvation by being suckled by a she-wolf. "Anyone who bears so great a name is surely destined for greatness," his father and mother assured him over and over.

A rural mail carrier at age 16, Brinkley spent much time dreaming about great things a 20th-century Romulus could do. Having determined that medicine was the coming thing, he decided to study it by mail since he was unable to attend college.

By 1911 Brinkley was an "undergraduate doctor," by permission of the North Carolina Board of Medical Examiners. Later he earned his medical degree by mail from the Eclectic Medical University of Kansas City.

Arkansas was one of the few states willing to honor a diploma from Eclectic as a valid M.D. degree. Once he was recognized in Arkansas, Dr. Brinkley used reciprocal agreements among states to build a pyramid of licenses in Tennessee, Connecticut, and Kansas. That enabled him to open a practice in Milford, Kansas, late in 1917. Milford had no hospital and no nearby doctors to ask embarrassing questions.

For years Brinkley had read about the ancients from whom his name had come. He learned that many cultures considered the goat the most sexually potent of animals. He pondered legends about gods who took on the form of goats and mated with the daughters of men. That led him to what he announced as a medical breakthrough without precedent.

"I learned to transplant goat glands," he said. "A childless patient from Wakefield went home and began chasing all the farm women. Within ten months, his wife, Dora, had a baby!"

Brinkley had found a medical pot of gold.

After he made his announcement, seven other males practically stood in line for the surgery. Each paid two hundred dollars for goat glands. Quickly borrowing money, the transplanted Tar Heel built a fifty-bed hospital. Then he won a Texas license by reciprocity with Arkansas.

Newspapers soon were running feature stories about his work. Since the "great surgeon" refused to reveal details about his astonishing new technique, the stories were rather vague. He told reporters rivals would steal his business if they knew exactly how he functioned.

By 1921 a steady stream of males was pouring into Dr. Brinkley's clinic in Milford, Kansas. The price of goat testicles rose steadily, peaked briefly at $750 a pair, and then doubled. Many Monday mornings found fifty men waiting for their operations.

Publicity soon brought the American Medical Association into action, and "Goat-gland Brinkley," as he was widely called, was charged with misrepresentation, outright fraud, and "gross immorality." When Brinkley lost his Kansas license, he quickly rebounded in Mexico. Eventually State Department pressure forced the closure of station XER, although Dr. Brinkley kept most of his luxury possessions.

A trickle of lawsuits grew into a stream. Eventually the

Twenty thousand people protested closing of Brinkley's radio station. [TEXAS STATE LIBRARY]

man who had parlayed a myth into a take of at least ten million dollars filed for bankruptcy.

While waiting for the federal court in San Antonio to act, John Romulus Brinkley ran for the U. S. Senate. Opponents called him "the greatest charlatan in the history of medicine," but many of his patients still swore by him.

Brinkley might have made it to Washington, had it not been for a lanky ex-teacher. Although he was world famous, Dr. Brinkley was beaten at the polls by a nearly unknown fellow by the name of Lyndon B. Johnson.

2

Wright Brothers Started Over En Route to Kitty Hawk

"Will, you insisted we had to have the right wind. That has put us on the way to Kitty Hawk," Orville Wright reminded his older brother as they rode the train from Ohio to North Carolina.

As Wilbur nodded in agreement, Orville continued, "We're going to have to scrap every idea anyone else has ever proposed."

Radical as Orville's idea was, the two bicycle mechanics from Dayton, Ohio, implemented it when they arrived at North Carolina's Outer Banks in September 1900. Discarding all they had learned, they took an entirely new direction as they began building a heavier-than-air machine.

Just eighteen months earlier, Wilbur had penned a fervent plea to the Smithsonian Institution. "I believe that simple flight at least is possible to man," he wrote. "I am an enthusiast, but not a crank. I wish to avail myself of all that is already known."

Poring over booklets and pamphlets and diagrams, the operators of the Wright Cycle Shop in Dayton arrived at a radical conclusion. For centuries men had been dreaming of flying like birds, and many had attempted the feat. All had failed, however, *because they tried to imitate the motions of a bird flapping its wings.*

"We can fly, and we will fly," Orville insisted. "But we will fly like a bird that uses the wind to soar with motionless wings."

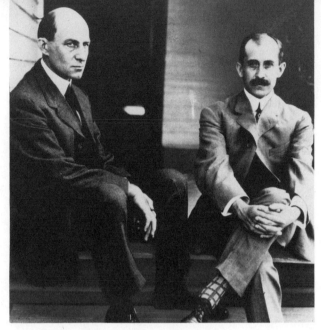

Wilbur Wright (l) with Orville (r) in 1910. They were almost inseparable until Wilbur's death in 1912. [NATIONAL AIR AND SPACE MUSEUM, SMITHSONIAN INSTITUTION]

Wilbur concurred, but only after insisting that they find the right spot to test their ideas.

Inquiries to the U. S. Weather Service brought a stack of publications. Some prospective sites were eliminated because there were too many hills and trees. Others were eliminated because winds were too variable.

Questioned by letter, Joseph J. Dosher reported in August 1900 that the beach at Kitty Hawk, North Carolina, was one mile wide and clear of trees for sixty miles. "Wind mostly from north and northeast September and October," he reported. "Sorry to say you could not rent a house here, so you will have to bring tents."

Postmaster William Tate, a commissioner of Currituck County, heard from Dosher that "Some fellows from Ohio think this would be a good place to test a flying machine."

Tate immediately sent a detailed report. At Kitty Hawk, he wrote, experimenters would find level sand covering an area one mile wide and five miles long "with a bare hill in center eighty feet high, not a tree or bush anywhere to break the evenness of the wind current. Our winds are always steady, generally from ten to twenty miles velocity per hour."

The brothers' first experiments in North Carolina, using gliders, were not dramatically successful. They were not totally unsuccessful, either. Soon they had expanded their vision to include using a motor to propel their machine.

Each year they returned to Kill Devil Hill, edging closer to flight. Money, however, was scarce. They seldom had net profits of three thousand dollars a year from their bicycle business, so they skimped, substituted, and improvised. A Dayton tinsmith made for them a gasoline tank about three inches in diameter and twelve inches in length. They modified bicycle hubs to fashion wheels and built a "launching track" from scrap lumber at a cost of four dollars.

Scoffers derided them as geese, ridiculing Wilbur and Orville for always wearing stiff white starched collars complete with neckties.

With Orville at the controls, a heavier-than-air machine flies for the first time. At right Wilbur watches intently. [NORTH CAROLINA DEPARTMENT OF ARCHIVES AND HISTORY]

Starched collar, necktie and all, Orville took off against a twenty-seven miles-per-hour wind on the morning of December 17, 1903. Their 605-pound *Kitty Hawk Flyer* was airborne for twelve seconds at a speed of about thirty-one miles per hour before it landed 120 feet from the take-off point.

On the train headed back to Dayton, the jubilant brothers agreed that the *Flyer* was likely to change the world nature of warfare. Later they confessed that had they been offered ten thousand dollars for all rights at the time, it "might have been too tempting to refuse."

*   *   *

Mankind was ushered into the air age at a point that had special meaning for native Americans. For generations coastal Indians had come every Fall to hunt migrating flocks of geese. The site of their "Killy Honk" hunt became the white man's Kitty Hawk.

A strange twist of fate, indeed!

Jocular post card sent to Orville by Will when the younger brother made headlines by setting new records. [WRIGHT STATE UNIVERSITY]

3

They Called Elizabeth Blackwell "Mad or Bad"

"Women and children—most of them, anyway—would welcome you," agreed John Dickinson, the clergy-man-physician of Asheville, North Carolina. "Many men—perhaps most of them—will view things in a different light. If you persist in your goal of becoming a doctor, you must be prepared to pay the price."

"I realize that!" interrupted Elizabeth Blackwell, the twenty-five-year-old teacher who had been Dr. Dickinson's pupil. Local tradition declares that she seized Dickinson's black bag and marched up and down the room, bag in hand. "I'll do whatever it takes! I'll pay whatever price is demanded!"

Born near Bristol, England, and brought to the United States by parents at about age ten, Elizabeth had studied under private tutors in early childhood. Then her father's fortunes had waned in their new country, and his death in 1838 left the family in poverty.

Elizabeth and two of her sisters opened a private school in Cincinnati. Later she taught in Henderson, Kentucky, before moving to North Carolina.

It was while teaching in Asheville that she began reading pamphlets and books about medicine. Soon she turned to John Dickinson for help. He guided her reading, and at intervals borrowed books from his brother in Charleston, South Carolina.

At first, he had regarded Elizabeth's interest as a hobby. When she declared her intention to win an M.D. degree,

Dr. Elizabeth Blackwell (far side of carriage), age 91, in a New York City suffrage parade.

he became deeply concerned. No female had ever been granted that degree.

Elizabeth insisted that she wouldn't stop without achieving her goal; so Dickinson sent her from the mountains to the sea, to his brother in Charleston. Dr. Samuel Dickinson, an instructor at Charleston Medical College, tutored her without charge.

When Ms. Blackwell applied to the School of Medicine at Harvard University, officials didn't take the letter seriously. "Clearly, she is either mad or bad," they concluded.

Rejected at Harvard, Elizabeth applied to Yale and then to Bowdoin. Next she tried every medical school in New York City, followed by applications to every school in Philadelphia.

Only when she had been turned down by these medical schools of national prominence did she begin applying to less well-known ones. Her thirtieth application went to the medical college of Geneva, New York.

There, officials sidestepped the issue of her sex. They polled members of the student body—some of whom probably considered the question a joke—and were surprised that a majority said they'd be willing to have a woman among their number.

In 1847, at age 36, Blackwell began her studies at Geneva, a school later incorporated into Syracuse University.

Many students, including some who had voted to admit her, refused to speak to her. Others harrassed her. Townsfolk ridiculed her openly, and professors initially barred "a member of the tender sex" from classroom anatomical demonstrations.

Incredibly, on January 29, 1849, she graduated with the highest academic record in her class. Yet she flatly refused to take part in the commencement procession. "It would be unladylike for me to participate," she said.

No clinic or hospital would give her a place on a staff; so she went to Paris for additional study at a famous maternity hospital. Then she did additional study at St. Bartholomew's in London.

Encouraged by Florence Nightingale and Oliver Wendell Holmes, America's first female M.D. went to New York City. There she found financial backing and launched an infirmary for women and children. Eventually it grew into a teaching institution for women.

First of its kind anywhere, the Women's Medical College of 1868 aroused so much opposition that its founder reacted by becoming a militant suffragette, remaining active in the movement for women's rights until her death.

Until the rise of the modern women's movement, Blackwell's feat had been largely forgotten. Today she is nearly universally revered, not simply for having been the first of her kind, but because she refused to quit when most persons—male or female—would have given up.

4

Original Siamese Twins Reared Families in Carolina

"Hurry!" Eng Bunker urged his wife in the pre-dawn hours of a January day in 1874. "There's something badly wrong!"

One look was enough to tell her the worst. Chang—Eng's Siamese twin—was dead.

Eyes dilated with terror, Eng cried, "Then my last hour is come! May the Lord have mercy on my soul!" Three hours later, Eng joined his twin brother in death.

A recently discovered autopsy report gave the verdict that modern science accepts. Eng died of fright. Joined to Chang's corpse, Eng's terror triggered his own death.

Connected by a mostly cartilaginous band, Chang and Eng were the original Siamese twins. Generations after their death, they remain far and away the best known.

Abel Coffin, skipper of a Yankee clipper ship, had discovered the pair on a visit to Bangkok. He instantly saw commercial opportunities and arranged with their mother for a "settlement" that nearly amounted to a purchase.

"I have two Chinese Boys seventeen years old," Coffin wrote to his daughter Susan. "They enjoy good health. I hope they will prove valuable as a curiosity."

Brought to Boston, the teenagers created a sensation. Coffin next decided to exhibit them where the real money was, in Europe.

Britain's famed Royal College of Surgeons invited Chang and Eng to tea, then the members eagerly exam-

26

ined them, sure they were a fraud. But the conjoined twins, as they are now called, baffled scholars. Pronounced authentic, Chang and Eng attracted 300,000 paying customers in England alone.

It was the London *Times* that first incorrectly called them "Siamese." A news story of November 1829 told readers that "Paris papers have announced that the Sardinian girl with two heads is dead. The Siamese twins will therefore have a clear field in France."

At that time their combined weight was just 180 pounds, yet they were so agile they could defeat four ordinary men in a rope-pulling contest. Although they could walk only side-by-side, they often took jaunts of six to eight miles. To sleep, they had to lie face-to-face.

Trouble between the curiosities and their manager came to a head on May 11, 1832, on their twenty-first birthday. They agreed to stay with Coffin for the rest of the month, but then they would go into business for themselves.

Nimble-minded and already proficient in English, the conjoined twins toured much of the United States on their

Chang (l) and Eng (r) with their wives and two of their twenty-two children.

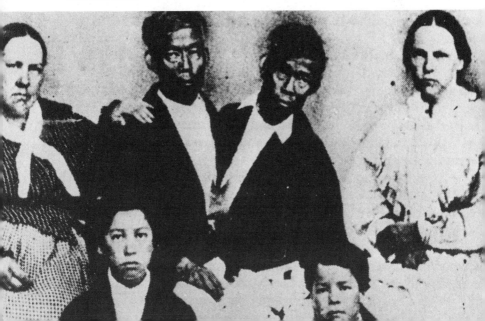

own. They usually charged fifty cents per person for admission to an "exhibition."

Showman P. T. Barnum then signed the brothers to a contract and for five years they drew more customers to his famous American Museum than did any other performers. They lived in frugal style and managed to put aside savings of about fifty thousand dollars.

Applying for U. S. citizenship, they were baffled when a clerk told them they had to have a surname. A stranger who overheard the conversation introduced himself to the twins as Fred Bunker and offered his name to the immigrants. This made it possible for them to win their citizenship.

Only strong-willed men would have considered marriage in such circumstances. Chang and Eng let it be known they'd gladly share their savings with "the right two girls."

They found Sarah and Adelaide Yates, from Wilkes County, North Carolina. Since they had decided to give up show business in favor of normal lives, after their marriage at the Baptist Church, they selected land in Surry County. There they built houses one mile apart.

For the next twenty-five years they lived near Mt. Airy. Except when on tour, they followed a strict schedule: three days at Chang's house with Adelaide, then three days at Eng's house with Sarah.

"Adelaide and I had the first child!" Chang liked to brag. "A fine boy—perfectly normal!"

Their son was followed by two more boys and seven girls. Eng and Sarah had seven boys plus five girls.

According to Dr. Robert Hollingsworth, though Chang contracted severe bronchitis, he insisted upon going to Eng's house at the customary time. It was there that he died of complications from illness—and his brother of fright.

Medical specialists today insist that Chang and Eng's bond was not that complex. Had modern surgical techniques been available then, it would have been a simple job to separate the brothers.

5

"Poorest of the Vanderbilts" Built Largest Mansion

At his father's death in 1885, George Washington Vanderbilt found himself almost impoverished, by family standards. As the youngest son, George received merely five million dollars, plus a trust fund of the same amount from his father's two-hundred-million-dollar estate.

William H. Vanderbilt was following the pattern established by dynasty founder Cornelius, widely known as "Commodore." At his death, just eight years before that of William, the Commodore had left him 90 percent of his $100 million. From generation to generation the first-born son served as head of the family and guardian of its fortune.

George already had inherited about $2.5 million from his grandfather. Yet at age twenty-three, the youngest male Vanderbilt had ideas far bigger than his assets.

Educated by private tutors, he spent much of his youth in Europe and was a master of eight languages. Uninterested in the world of high finance, he decided to make his mark in another arena.

In the year of his father's death young George visited the mountains of western North Carolina. Like most who see them for the first time, he was intoxicated. Unlike the typical visitor from up East, he picked a particularly spectacular site near Asheville and decided to build himself a mountain house there.

George's oldest brother, Cornelius, moved into immediate control of a fortune ten times that of George. Soon he was a director of thirty-four railroad companies. William

Childhood home of George W. Vanderbilt on New York's Fifth Avenue. [NEW YORK PUBLIC LIBRARY]

K., second in seniority among males, inherited nearly one hundred million dollars.

Their serious-minded younger brother who'd fallen in love with the Smokies was eager to become a resident of North Carolina. With seven million dollars cash in hand, he set out to build a house along the lines of those he had enjoyed most in Europe.

The chateau he envisaged as the Biltmore House would require a proper setting. So young Vanderbilt bought up about 125,000 acres nearby, with Mt. Pisgah included in the tract.

Richard Morris Hunt, finest Beaux Arts architect of the era, gladly tackled the assignment of planning the most magnificent country home in North America. He chose Indiana limestone as a building material and did not stop until he had sketched plans for the 254th room.

Frederick Law Olmsted, revered in Atlanta for having drawn up the master plan for Druid Hills and nationally acclaimed for having designed New York's Central Park, said he couldn't possibly prepare an acceptable landscape plan unless he had at least 250 acres with which to work.

That suited George Washington Vanderbilt. After all, Versailles and Fontainebleau wouldn't be architectural gems without proper settings.

By the time Hunt and Olmsted were reasonably well satisfied with their work, their employer was committed to spending more than seven million dollars.

The Biltmore has a library with a seventy-foot ceiling whose shelves are lined with fine leather-bound volumes. Its tapestry gallery is seventy-five feet in length. A banquet hall that measures seventy-two feet by forty-two feet has such acoustical qualities that persons sitting at opposite ends of the vast table can converse without raising their voices.

The Biltmore house.

Each of the thirty-four main bedrooms has its own bath. An indoor swimming pool has seventeen private dressing rooms.

Landscape artist Olmstead delighted at having created "America's finest British garden." To keep it at its best, gardeners annually plant and dig up 40,000 tulip bulbs.

When completed after five years of work by one thousand men, the Biltmore had just the right atmosphere to make King Louis XIV feel at home, although it was equipped with some of Thomas Edison's earliest filament light bulbs.

In order to experience Europe at its finest a few hours from home, more than 650,000 paying visitors come annually to the house George Washington Vanderbilt erected with almost his entire inheritance. Immense fortunes held by his older brothers have been largely dissipated, but the Biltmore has gained worldwide fame. Listed as the world's largest private home in *Guiuness Book of World Records*, it could not be built today for $50,000,000—even if the skilled craftsmen who worked on it were available.

George Washington Vanderbilt as a student.

6

Schoolboy Paid Millions for Borrowed Books

"It's the absolute, unvarnished truth," declares Duke University archivist Dr. William E. King. "A program by which Duke lent books by mail during the Great Depression later triggered gifts to the university of more than $24 million. J. B. Fuqua, chairman of the board of the Fortune 500 corporation that bears his name, is the man who is responsible."

Fuqua's boyhood was spent in rural Prince Edward County, Virginia, in the aftermath of World War I. Very early he noticed that "all the big houses in town were owned by bankers." That helped him decide to go into business. Setting goals for himself of becoming a millionaire by age thirty and eventually of heading a billion-dollar corporation, Fuqua achieved both, but not without surmounting formidable obstacles.

At age fourteen he invested twenty-five cents in a book of instructions about ham radio operations. From that little book, he learned enough to win a ham license.

"Radio proved fascinating beyond the power of words to describe," he said later. "I saw that if I was to get anywhere in the field, I'd have to learn a lot. That meant just one thing: a program of self-education."

Launched on the program he had devised for himself, the youngster stumbled upon good news. Far to the south in Durham, North Carolina, Duke University was willing to lend books by mail.

Fuqua first borrowed volumes about radio. Then he dug

into others dealing with banking and finance. Soon he decided to go into the technical side of radio, with the long-range goal of "moving into the business side, where the money is." After graduating from high school, Fuqua won a berth in the merchant marine as a radio operator. He stayed with that job for two years. During that time he concentrated his energies on saving as much money as possible. In order to enter the business world, he would need money, and in order to save anything, he had to live frugally.

J. B. Fuqua. [Fuqua Industries]

Changing jobs, but still saving all he could, the largely self-taught youngster launched his first big research project working for a Columbia, South Carolina, radio station. He searched for "just the right spot at which a new station would turn a profit quickly."

"Aha!" he concluded one day, "I've found the spot—Augusta, Georgia."

Names of potential investors were found at the Augusta Chamber of Commerce. Then he persuaded three of them to put up ten thousand dollars with which to launch radio station WGAC.

For his efforts, Fuqua got 10 percent ownership, plus the job of managing the station. Later he launched WJBF-TV in Augusta.

When he married Augustan Dorothy Chapman, he was twenty-seven years old and was one-tenth of the way toward his goal of becoming a millionaire.

He already had started upon what became a life-long career, buying corporations, often re-structuring and selling them for a quick profit. His boyhood ambition of becoming a millionaire was achieved at age thirty-five, five years behind schedule.

Fuqua found time to serve three terms in Georgia's House of Representatives and one term in the state senate. He was chairman of the state Democratic Party from 1962 to 1966.

By then he realized he would have to choose between business and politics. Friends and relatives knew his decision before he announced it. "I'm going to give Fuqua Industries everything I've got," he declared.

Soon he went public with Fuqua Industries stock, and in just four years the company reached the Fortune 500 list.

That's when *Fortune* magazine sent reporters to prepare a full-length article about the man who, without a college degree, was shaking up the world of American business.

Duke University's librarian at the time read the *Fortune* article and sent aides to the engineering library. There they found books still holding cards with Fuqua's name on them.

As a gesture of good will, the librarian sent Fuqua a radio handbook he had borrowed. Soon Fuqua agreed to serve on the Board of Visitors of the Graduate School of Business Administration.

Founded at Duke in 1969, the business school had no building, few students, and little reputation. J. B. Fuqua, who hadn't spent a day on campus until he came as a visitor, set out to help change things.

In 1980 he made Duke a gift of land in Houston, Texas, along with other property and cash. Today the value of that no-strings-attached gift is well above $20 million. That made it the largest gift Duke had ever received up to that time from anyone other than founder J. B. Duke. Grateful trustees of the university created the Fuqua School of Business and recruited Fuqua as a member of the board.

Soon R. David Thomas, founder of the Wendy's restaurant chain, became a friend of Duke through his friendship with Fuqua. He pledged four million dollars to the school of business.

With Thomas's gift, the direct return from lending books to an aspiring farm boy passed twenty-four million dollars. Not bad, even by J. B. Fuqua's standards!

7

William Bartram Was Decades Ahead of Audubon

Indians called him Puc-Puggy, or "Flower Hunter." Benjamin Franklin fondly referred to him as "my dear son." George Washington, John Adams, and Thomas Jefferson subscribed to his pioneer book describing his travels in the Carolinas, Georgia, and other areas of the South.

Born in Pennsylvania in 1739, from early childhood William Bartram was fascinated by birds, flowers, and animals. Before he learned to read, he had spent many hours looking at engravings in books used by his father, a noted botanist.

At age fourteen William began to draw birds. Plants followed, then animals. He showed such skill that Benjamin Franklin offered to teach him the art of printing.

Instead of entering Franklin's shop, young Bartram studied under Charles Thomson who later served as secretary of the Continental Congress. By 1756, when he was seventeen, noted scientists were praising the quality of his drawings and paintings.

During the next decade he made a long field trip to the deep South under the expert leadership of his father. In that era when no wildlife artist was self-supporting, he was unable to launch out on his own until he found a patron.

Then John Fothergill of London learned of the American's work. A wealthy physician who cultivated exotic plants on his estate at Upton in Essex, Fothergill was eager

William Bartram. [PORTRAIT BY CHARLES
WILLSON PEALE]

for rare specimens from America. So he agreed to pay Bartram's expenses, plus fifty pounds a year. Backed so gener-
ously, the American left Philadelphia for Carolina early in
1773, aboard the ship *Charles-Town Packet.*

During four years in southeastern North America, Bartram, the first trained wildlife artist to visit the region,
sent a stream of seeds, specimens, and drawings to England. Puc-Puggy, as Indian guides called him, made detailed notes in his daily journal. Both of the Carolinas,
said Bartram, were awesome and sublime.

More than any creature he had ever seen, the alligator
excited a sense of awe in Bartram. Coastal waters and
rivers were full of these beasts, who often threshed

furiously "with tail brandished high." Bartram noted with a mixture of surprise and relief that no alligators were to be seen in the Savannah River north of Augusta.

Every morning at sunrise, he reported, "the dreaded voice of the allegators" literally shook the land. Even without sounds of bellowing, sketches of alligators excited fear in England. After a look at Bartram's alligators, one Londoner decided he preferred his "old smoaky apartments in Grub-Street" to coastal North America.

Bartram could hardly believe his eyes when he saw a turkey gobbler fully three feet high, "a stately beautiful bird who seemed not insensible of his splendid appearance."

In his role as botanist, Bartram painted the *Franklinia Altamaha*. First seen by his father and named for Benjamin Franklin, this flower is now extinct in the wild, but it grows in botanical gardens, thanks to seeds provided by John and William Bartram.

A native fruit also excited Bartram's admiration. His sketch of "wild semmons" is a botanical first; no one had ever before depicted persimmons.

Somewhere on a river believed to have been the French Broad, a settler penned a description of Bartram.

> He is as wild-looking as any creature of the fields or woods. Most who have seen him consider him to be daft [insane]. He says he lives off the land, goes many days without sleeping in a cabin.
>
> At every opportunity, he stops and takes out paper plus charcoal or brush and paint. Common, everyday wild things intrigue him so much that he depicts them.

As a result of Bartram's passion, today we can view the flora and fauna of Carolina as they appeared more than 200 years ago.

8

Blackbeard Refused to Die

"Load with scrap iron and swan!" shouted Blackbeard.

Crew members who jumped to obey their commander needed no explanation. Use of swan shot, alleged to "whistle like a dying swan," meant that they would fight to the death.

Two big sloops, spotted as they moved into Pamlico Sound, had worked their way to Ocracoke Island, North Carolina. Now—in the pre-dawn hours on November 22, 1718—they appeared to be stranded in treacherous shoals. It was the best possible situation for an all-out attack by pirates.

With swan shot whistling from big guns loaded to their muzzles, Blackbeard and his men used rowboats to reach a twenty-gun sloop commanded by Lt. Robert Maynard of the British Royal Navy.

They boarded in pre-dawn hours and quickly identified their foes as sailors based somewhere in Virginia, probably on frigates in the James River. Cursing, screaming, and wielding huge cutlasses, the pirates killed twenty-nine enemies in a matter of minutes.

When the pirates found nobody with the commander's rank on board, they retreated to Teach's Hole, named for their leader whose real name was probably Edward Teach (or Edward Thatch). There they planned a second assault.

Blackbeard knew the importance of a bizarre and distinctive appearance. As brigands of the sea go, he was sec-

40

ond or third rate, but he more than compensated for
sloppy seamanship by a never-to-be-forgotten appearance.

Locks of his long black hair and beard were twisted into
tiny pigtails that were bound with strips of colored cloth.
A leather belt across his shoulders and chest carried two
braces of pistols, often three.

In preparing to board an enemy ship, he would put a
sword in his huge right hand, clench a two-foot knife between his teeth, and tie slow-burning matches to pigtails
around his forehead.

His popular name stemmed from the "immense quan-
tity of coal-black hair which, like a frightful meteor, covered his entire countenance."

Probably, but not positively, born in or near Bristol, England, he took to the sea during the War of the Spanish
Succession. When peace treaties were signed, he became
a pirate.

British authorities offered amnesty to brigands who
would take their vessels to the Bahamas and turn themselves in. Many took advantage of the offer, but Blackbeard thumbed his nose at it and headed for the Carolinas.

By the time he reached Charleston, many of his men
were sick. Blackbeard sent a tender into the harbor, de-
manding a medicine chest and threatening to kill hos-
tages if refused. According to respected authorities,
"magistrates of Charleston meekly complied."

It may have been that incident that persuaded the pirate
leader to take a serious look at public authority. Whatever
the case, he sought and found a man who was willing to
help him—for a price.

Royal Governor Charles Eden headed North Carolina—
a separate colony only since 1711. Along with the provin-
cial collector, Tobias Knight, he agreed to give the pirates
protection, and they established headquarters on Ocracoke Island.

From a single captured French ship, Eden received
sixty hogsheads of sugar; Knight was given twenty. Eden
is said to have performed the ceremony in which Black-

beard took a Carolina girl as his fourteenth wife.

Subjected to pillage by the protected pirates, planters and settlers turned to Virginia for help. Responding to their plea, Lt. Gov. Alexander Spotswood decided to use men from the Royal Navy to wipe out "the monstrous nest of seafaring vipers" in Carolina. Spotswood's orders led to the bloody November engagement of 1718.

Surveying the deck of the stricken sloop through his glass, Blackbeard saw no sign of movement. Dressed in all his splendor, he boarded a second time.

At that moment, Lt. Robert Maynard, who had been hiding in the hold, emerged and shot the pirate through the head, and Blackbeard's men beat a hasty retreat. While they were still in sight, Maynard cut off the head of their leader and dumped his body into the water.

Eyewitnesses later swore that the headless body circled the sloop three or four times, then disappeared into a slow dive. Legend asserts British authorities got Blackbeard's head, but his body continues to prowl the beaches in order to guard buried gold.

At Bath a summer outdoor drama, *Blackbeard, Knight of the Black Flag,* keeps memories of America's most colorful pirate very much alive.

Blackbeard's last fight. [NORTH CAROLINA DEPARTMENT OF ARCHIVES AND HISTORY]

9

Dorothea Dix Shook Up the Lawmakers

At age forty-six, Dorothea Dix was "an invalid in the process of recuperation." She had staged many a one-woman fight; more often than not, she had been victorious.

Now she was ready to square off for one of her toughest bouts—against the North Carolina legislature.

Two factors boosted her chances. Of the original thirteen colonies, only Delaware and North Carolina were without institutions for care of the insane. Dorothea's appeal to state pride would be enhanced by her growing national reputation, which would cause at least one major newspaper to back her crusade.

She also had heavy liabilities. In an era when most women avoided public controversy, she was noted for stirring it up. What's more, she hailed from "way Up North" in Maine—in the era when North/South friction was mounting.

To make matters worse, the self-styled woman reformer was known to be determined to ask for an impossible sum: $100,000. That amount of money would double the budget of the state.

Arriving in 1848 without a single aide, Dorothea Dix followed a practice that had worked elsewhere. First she spent weeks traveling through major population centers gathering case histories of brutal treatment meted out to the mentally ill.

Then she enlisted a powerful friend, the editor of the

Dorothea Dix as portrayed on a
commemorative stamp. [U.S. POSTAL
SERVICE]

Raleigh Register. By early December, the newspaper was
praising her as "a high-souled, earnest, persevering
woman" who was working wholeheartedly for "a most
noble charity; that of procuring a home for the most
wretched of her fellow beings."

In spite of that tribute, veteran capital watchers didn't
give the upcoming "Memorial by Miss Dix" any hope.
Lawmakers were primarily concerned with fostering the
state's infant railroad system.

Incredibly, though, railroad backer John W. Ellis of
Rowan County sponsored the bill that the woman from
"Up North" wanted. Under its terms, the legislature
would provide funds with which to erect an asylum. Lu-
natics would then be transferred from county poorhouses
and jails to "an institution offering the most modern medical treatment known."

Though the Ellis bill was believed doomed before it
could reach the floor, Dorothea Dix remained in Raleigh

and actively lobbied for its passage. Staying at Raleigh's Mansion House hotel, she spent much of her spare time attending to another guest, Mrs. James C. Dobbin.

In spite of her efforts, Mrs. Dobbin died on December 18. Momentarily giving up her political activity, Ms. Dix traveled to Fayetteville for the funeral. Richard A. Faust, who meticulously investigated the work of Dorothea Dix in North Carolina, pointed out that she knew Mrs. Dobbin was the wife of an influential legislator.

As expected, the "asylum bill" was voted down when it reached the floor of the legislature on December 21. According to Faust's account, "at this point, chance and the result of Dorothea's kindness brought success."

Returning from the funeral of his wife, James Dobbin made a stirring appeal for reconsideration of the bill calling for erection of an asylum. His influence led to development of a compromise.

Quick action by the House, on the heels of the Dobbin appeal of December 22, brought an overwhelmingly positive vote. Dorothea Dix was hailed as having "presented North Carolina with the finest Christmas present on record."

Commissioners of the new insane hospital of North Carolina wanted to name the institution for her. She adamantly refused. Then, yielding a bit, she agreed to let them name the site for her grandfather, Dr. Elijah Dix.

Dix Hill became a byword in Carolina. Then the legislature acted once more. During the centennial celebration of the first patient's admission in 1956, lawmakers renamed the Dix Hill Asylum as Dorothea Dix Hospital.

Dorothea Dix was instrumental in founding institutions for the care of the mentally ill in a dozen states and many cities. Only two in the nation perpetuate her name.

Frail in childhood and an invalid during a period as a young woman, she was drafted to teach a Sunday School class in a Massachusetts jail when a pastor failed to keep an appointment. Finding terrible conditions among the insane confined there, she was so shocked that she forgot her own infirmities and launched a one-woman crusade that lasted for decades.

10

No One Ever Wielded a Cane Like Preston Brooks

"Pierce Butler and his kind deserve no voice in this august body!" cried U. S. Senator Charles Sumner of Massachusetts.

Fellow lawmakers who had been dozing, bored by the long-drawn debate over Kansas, were shaken awake by startled colleagues. Every man in the house knew and usually obeyed the unwritten law by which no senator was permitted to criticize another by name.

Having breached the "gentleman's code" that had prevailed for decades, Sumner made no apology. Instead, the violently partisan abolitionist kept the floor. He spoke for what seemed an eternity, heaping abuse upon slave owners in general and Senator Pierce Butler of South Carolina in particular.

Few partisan issues in American politics have been debated so furiously as the Kansas–Nebraska Act of 1854. Stephen A. Douglas, "the little giant" of American politics, saw in it what he considered to be a workable compromise on the slavery issue.

Let new territories be organized, said Douglas, without specifying whether or not slavery would be legal. Once settlers establish themselves, permit them the liberty of deciding the issue for themselves.

It was the notion of "squatter sovereignty" to which Sumner and fellow foes of slavery violently objected. They wanted slavery outlawed in every new territory.

Men from slave states hoped that by permitting popular sovereignty they could hold their own in the U. S. Senate.

If the delicate balance in that body should be destroyed, the nation would disintegrate, or would be plunged into civil war.

Senator Pierce Butler was attacked by Sumner because he was reputed to own more slaves—and bigger plantations—than any other member of the lawmaking body.

On the day of Sumner's personal attack, Butler was not present to speak for himself in defense of his character or his views. But one of his nephews, who also was influential in the nation's capital, was close at hand.

Preston S. Brooks, born at Edgefield, South Carolina, and a veteran of the Mexican War, had been elected to the House of Representatives in 1852 at age thirty-three. Six feet tall and widely considered the handsomest man in the House, he was regarded as gracious and gentle, except when angry.

Charles Sumner's vitriolic attack upon his absent uncle made Preston Brooks fighting mad. According to the South Carolinian's own account, he sent a message to the senator from Massachusetts. In it he demanded an apology. When no apology was forthcoming, Brooks stalked the streets of the capital, but failed to find Sumner.

Two days after Sumner's attack, the congressman made his way to the Senate chamber at adjournment. As law-

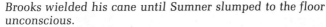

Brooks wielded his cane until Sumner slumped to the floor unconscious.

Senator Charles Sumner.

makers filed out, Brooks worked his way to Sumner's desk.

Having reached his foe, Brooks lifted his gutta percha cane and began clubbing Sumner. By the time the cane snapped, Sumner was slumping to the floor, apparently unconscious.

Senators and aides grabbed Brooks and held his arms, but it was too late. Sumner had received injuries from which he never fully recovered. "Senator Butler's honor has been restored," said Congressman Brooks tersely.

Fellow lawmakers took a different view of his violent actions. A special investigating committee named to consider the incident favored the expulsion of Brooks from the House. Put to the vote, the recommendation failed to get the required two-thirds majority.

Brooks, a noted orator, made an impassioned speech defending his conduct; then he resigned. Constituents promptly re-elected him to the seat he had vacated.

At the University of Georgia, students took up a collection and bought a new gold-headed cane for Brooks. Texas admirers sent him a gold-handled cowhide.

Aaron Burlingame of Massachusetts, a colleague in the House of Representatives, challenged him to a duel on the Canadian side of Niagara Falls. Brooks laughed, taunting his foe, "You might as well have named Boston Common as the place of meeting."

Veteran capital watchers say that nothing in our nation's history quite matches Congressman Brooks's response to Senator Sumner's insult.

PART TWO:

These Had Raw Courage

Submarine Hunley on Charleston dock.

11

Every Voyage of the *Hunley* Was a Suicide Mission

"Until about 8:45 P.M. it was a routine evening," wrote J. R. Crosby, acting master of the warship USS *Housatonic*. His vessel was on blockade duty in the Charleston, South Carolina, harbor on February 17, 1864.

"Suddenly the lookout spotted something. It was about one hundred yards away, and at first looked like a huge log. But it was moving too fast to be drifting with the tide.

"Our chain was slipped, the engine was backed, and all hands were called to quarters. Then the torpedo hit.

"It struck the *Housatonic* forward of the mizzenmast, on the starboard side. With our after pivot gun bearing to port, we were unable to fire.

"Within a minute after the explosion took place, we started down—with our vessel sinking stern first and heeling to port. Five members of our valiant crew died at once."

Crosby's record constitutes the only on-the-scene account of the world's first kill by a submarine. Not until decades later, early in World War I, was another warship sunk by an underwater craft.

Confederates built their submarine at Mobile, Alabama, and named her for designer Horace Hunley of New Orleans. An old steam boiler about twenty-five feet long and four feet wide provided the shell of the CSS *Hunley*.

Cut in two lengthwise, the boiler was strengthened by twelve-inch iron strips. Ballast tanks, equipped with sea cocks and force pumps, were riveted across the stern and bow.

There was only one source of illumination, a big candle. When it began to flicker, crew members were warned that oxygen was running low.

Power for the craft that some derisively called "the fish" came from Confederate muscles. Each of the eight crew members helped turn the shaft to which a small propeller was attached.

From the outset, builders of the *Hunley* knew their goal, to break the Federal blockade of Charleston harbor. So the thirty-five-foot craft was loaded on two flatcars and shipped to the port city early in 1864.

Only volunteers were accepted for duty inside "the fish." A trial run at Mobile had ended in tragedy; someone had failed to turn a sea cock, and every man in the *Hunley* died.

Once in Charleston, Lt. George E. Dixon, who had helped to build the craft, took command. With the man for whom she was named at the helm, "the fish" dived under the receiving ship CSS *Indian Chief.*

The *Hunley* failed to surface on the other side of the ship. It was a week before salvage crews pulled the sub from the bottom and found that, this time, the after valve had not been closed tightly.

In spite of the murderous record of "the fish," there was no scarcity of volunteers for her first mission against an enemy.

Confederate Gen. P. T. G. Beauregard, in command at Charleston, stipulated that for the sake of safety, the *Hunley* would have to resort to use of a spar torpedo. Lashed to a long pole, it projected from the bow of the craft.

When George Dixon scanned the harbor, he saw no shortage of targets; enemy vessels had tightened their grip upon Charleston. He picked a handsome sloop—rigged like a small frigate—and told his volunteers that it would make a fine prize.

A prize it was. Nearly everything ahead of the mainmast of the *Housatonic* was crumpled by the blast of the *Hunley's* torpedo. Even the rudder post and screw were blown away. From a distance of a few hundred yards, the

USS *Canadaigua* came to the rescue, so that 21 officers and 137 men from the *Housatonic* were saved.

Not until February 27 did Confederates learn that the big blockade ship had gone down. They knew the *Hunley* had not returned, but they didn't know that her torpedo had ripped the converted steam boiler open at the bow.

In trial runs and in her only assault upon an enemy, the *Hunley* claimed thirty-three Confederate lives. But she was one of the most unusual innovations of the Civil War and was the distant ancestor of today's nuclear-powered submarines.

A full-scale replica of the *Hunley* now sits in front of the Charleston Museum. Another replica, said to be somewhat more accurate, is displayed in the South Carolina Museum in Columbia. Differences between the two are not readily apparent to the casual viewer. Both replicas, viewed thoughtfully, bring overwhelming realization that men who manned the submarine placed the cause of their region above their own lives.

Hunley's *torpedo hits the* Housatonic.

12

Francis Asbury Rode the Long Trail

"I rode, I walked, I sweated, I trembled, and my old knees failed," Francis Asbury confided in his voluminous diary.

Having spent the night at Samuel Edney's cabin in Buncombe County's foothills, he was headed in the general direction of present-day Forest City, North Carolina.

"We had to cope with Little and Great Hunger mountains," he noted. "Now I know what Mills Gap is: one of the descents is like the roof of a house for nearly a mile."

Usually riding because the Blue Ridge Mountains had few trails usable even by a Jersey wagon, the man often called "the prophet on horseback" noted that he passed through South Carolina forty-six times and North Carolina sixty-three times.

"I seldom mount my horse for a ride of less distance than twenty miles," he observed.

Nearly always, at the end of a day he found a place where he could bring a few settlers together for a sermon and a prayer. Francis Asbury was a man with a mission; Methodist founder John Wesley had selected him to establish the new church in America—all America—and he intended to do exactly that.

Born in Staffordshire, England, in 1745, Asbury became an itinerant follower of Wesley at age twenty-two. With only three years' experience, he was handpicked to head the movement in the New World.

He could not have come to his new field at a worse time. Relations between the colonies and Britain, fre-

Francis Asbury.

A kneeling Francis Asbury is consecrated as the nation's first Methodist bishop.

quently bad, were getting worse by the month.

Somehow, Asbury managed to maintain his ties with John Wesley and with the Methodist movement in England throughout the American Revolution. But the church was not strong enough to withstand the move toward American nationalism.

Methodists of North America organized themselves as a separate body and in 1784 named Asbury as their first bishop. For the next thirty years he traveled continually.

Since whites had settled only the Atlantic seaboard, Asbury's trips from north to south and from south to north required that he frequently go over some of the roughest terrain in the young nation. After he had crossed the Appalachian Mountains half a dozen times, Asbury began speaking of these trips as "going over the Alps."

Many times he dismounted and led his horse; thickets

were so dense that animals could not penetrate them un-aided. Hence Methodism's first bishop became an expert at "bushing it." He confided in his diary that he was proud to show a young fellow how he could force his way through a thicket "and make the young saplings bend be-fore me, and twist and turn out of the way."

Through summer heat and winter cold, he rode nearly every day. He came to like sleet and snow, but the older he became the more he despised the ever-present mud.

Small wonder that Asbury suffered almost constantly from stomach and throat disorders, skin irritations, fe-vers, sore throat, boils, bronchitis, asthma, weak eyes, toothache, and even "galloping consumption." His favor-ite remedy was tartar emetic, but he often resorted to use of sage tea sweetened with loaf sugar and rose leaves. Oc-casionally he resorted to mustard plasters.

Asbury called Methodists of the region to an April 20, 1785, conference in this Louisberg, North Carolina, home.

Nights were—if possible—typically worse than the days. Frequently he was happy to sleep in a barn loft. "A plain, clean plank is preferable to most beds," he wrote. In most cabins persons slept three deep, producing frequent attacks of itch and almost nightly bouts with fleas.

An exception was the Shook house in Haywood County, North Carolina, where hospitality was warm, beds were fitted with clean sheets, and there were no insects. A historical marker not far from Clyde, North Carolina indicates the site of one of Francis Asbury's favorite stopping places.

"I hope I shall not live long after I am unable to travel," he once wrote. His wish was granted.

Until two years before his death, "the prophet of the long road" traveled almost annually from Maine's Androscoggin River to the Gulf of Mexico. As the nation expanded, he traveled from the Atlantic to the Mississippi River.

He preached 17,000 sermons, ordained 3,000 preachers, and personally superintended the Methodist movement during its period of most rapid expansion. Compared with Asbury's treks over the mountains, the short and dramatic "midnight ride of Paul Revere" was a Sunday School frolic.

13

Angelina Grimke Defied Charleston Tradition

"Stop waving the paper in my face and let me take a look at it," Angelina Grimke said. Her friend, James Bettle of Philadelphia, had rushed into her rooms flourishing a copy of the *Liberator*. Edited and published by William Lloyd Garrison, it was famous—or infamous—as an antislavery journal.

Angelina's pulse began to race. Face flushed, she found reading difficult.

"These are my words," she eventually said, "just as I wrote them. But I was not consulted about publication."

"Why? Oh, why?" stormed Bettle. "You are a woman—a woman from the aristocratic South, a woman from Charleston. Why?"

Wordless, Angelina pointed to the headline: Slavery and the Boston Riot. In May 1835, an antislavery convention had been refused the use of Faneuil Hall. One after another, seven churches then refused to open their facilities to abolitionists. When they persisted and found a meeting place, opponents formed a mob and a riot ensued.

Born and reared in a patrician family of Charleston, Angelina Grimke early formed strong views about slavery. She became convinced that unless slavery was abolished, America would be bathed in blood. Slave uprisings would rock the nation.

Her father, a wealthy, conservative justice of the South Carolina supreme court, owned so many slaves he was never sure of the exact head count. "A tender and reflec-

Masthead of The Liberator, the abolitionist newspaper that exploited Grimke's letter.

tive young woman," Angelina refused to accept the gift of a slave in childhood. Later she would not permit her father even to provide a body servant. Slavery was not only dangerous, she decided; it was morally wrong.

Had she remained in the cloistered life of Charleston, one of America's richest and most cosmopolitan cities, Angelina might never have voiced her views except to intimate friends.

However, a stay in Philadelphia at age twenty-seven created new questions. In time, she became a Quaker by choice, turning her back upon her Episcopalian rearing. Though she visited Charleston from time to time, it never again was home to her.

Living in Philadelphia and pondering the evils of slavery and the Boston riot, the shy, courteous, blue-eyed Charlestonian took pen in hand. After several days, she had a letter ready to send to Garrison, but several times she deferred posting it. Years later, she admitted, "I really did fear that he might publish it, but I had no idea he would use my name."

"I was compelled at this time to address thee," she wrote to editor Garrison. "I can hardly express to thee the deep and solemn interest with which I have viewed the violent proceedings of the last few weeks."

News that abolitionist J. Dresser had been publicly flogged may have been the catalyst that changed her from passive to active opposition to "the peculiar institution" of slavery.

"If persecution is the means which God has ordained for the accomplishment of *emancipation;* then, *let it come* . . . for it is my deep, solemn, deliberate conviction that *this is a cause worth dying for.*"

Publication of these sentiments meant cutting most or all existing ties. Her family would repudiate her, and Quakers would turn her out of their meeting because she hadn't shown proper discipline. Sarah, her beloved older sister whom she later converted to the cause of abolition, was initially so horrified at Angelina's actions that she did not communicate with her for weeks.

Her 1836 *Appeal to the Christian Women of the South* was so despised that many postmasters publicly burned copies of it.

In the City of Brotherly Love, she raised the hackles of civic leaders by advocating erection of a special hall for use by abolitionists. What's more, she helped to raise money for it.

Opening night saw the woman from Charleston a featured speaker in Philadelphia's new Pennsylvania Hall. Hecklers were on hand, and a mob gathered. Late that night the hall was burned to the ground.

Charleston had already disowned her most noted—or notorious—daughter. Philadelphia tolerated her but used sticks and stones and firebrands to tell her what she already knew: she was almost alone against a world in which most who didn't foster slavery openly tolerated it.

14

Gibson's General Store Shook and Swayed

Thomas Gibson studied the cards in his hand. The situation called for strategy, not rash action. Across the table from him, John Pipkin waited patiently. Hamp Adams and William Gibson, also sitting around the table, shuffled their feet as a signal calling for action.

Gibson reached for a card

Just as his hand touched the card, at about 9:30 P.M., a low-pitched and wavering moan made each player jerk bolt upright.

Pipkin, at age twenty-nine already a Marlboro County, South Carolina, commissioner, remembered warnings voiced by the preacher a few Sundays earlier. Since then he had doubted the wisdom of accepting the invitation to play cards in the second-floor storage room of Gibson's General Store.

Later, villagers of McColl, South Carolina, remembered that August 31, 1886, was the first day of the cotton ginning season. With pressure in the boiler low, dew probably settled on the whistle cord. That made it just heavy enough to release the steam that produced the eerie moan.

But for wielders of "the devil's calling cards" who'd refused to run, a supernatural sound was just the start. They'd barely stopped discussing the moan, whose nature they still didn't understand, when caskets stacked next to the outside wall began to shake and rattle.

Most general stores of the era kept caskets in stock. Like unopened bolts of cloth and kegs of nails, they were customarily stored on the second floor.

Refuges created a "tent city" in stricken Charleston.

The rattling caskets were simply too much for Pipkin, and he decided it was time to fold up and go home. Clearly, he was receiving a divine warning, or a threat from the devil himself.

Incredibly, the youthful county commissioner and his friends did not panic. They simply put up their cards, doused the light, and calmly walked down the steps and out the front door. Come daylight, they reasoned, they would get to the bottom of that unearthly noise and the rattling and shaking unlike anything they had ever experienced.

News—a bit of it, that is—reached the village before morning. Charleston had been hit by an earthquake—not a mild tremor, but a genuine earthquake. That's about all anyone in McColl knew until the morning train brought a few papers.

At 9:51 P.M., clocks in Charleston all stopped. One newspaper reporter said that "An awful roar bombarded my ears, and the strong-walled building shook as though an immeasurable power intended to tear it asunder."

Soon streets and parks were filled with terror-stricken

men, women, and children. A few tried to flee in small boats. An estimated 50,000 persons were trapped near the center of a major earthquake, later listed as the fifth most lethal in U. S. history.

More than 90 percent of the city's buildings were damaged. Twenty fires were roaring out of control; there was nothing to do except watch buildings burn to the ground. Even if water mains had not burst, firemen would have been helpless; every street was obstructed by rubble.

At Gibson's General Store in McColl the next day, the usual trickle of customers was augmented by a flood of curious people who wanted a firsthand look at "the place where the coffins rattled last night." Most who trudged up the steps to see for themselves shook their heads in wonder. "How on earth did John Pipkin and his buddies manage not to panic?" they asked.

The tale of raw courage on a fearful night has been transmitted orally in South Carolina for a century. Ruthie Pipkin of The Waynesville, North Carolina, *Mountaineer* may have been first to put this tale into print. Amended and amplified by her grandfather, it emerges, not as folk lore or fiction, but as an authentic account of actions in the face of fearful events no one in McColl could explain on the night they took place.

Henry W. Grady won national attention through his coverage of the Charleston earthquake.

15

Boy Hero of the Waxhaws Defied the British

Exactly where did pioneers establish a settlement that in time became a tiny village called Waxhaw? Respected authorities disagree on this point. Many insist it was in the area now encompassed by Lancaster County, North Carolina. Not so, say others, believing it lay just below the line dividing North Carolina from South Carolina.

Because Andrew Jackson spent his boyhood in the disputed settlement, the birthplace of our seventh president thus is claimed by both North and South Carolina.

The story of Andrew Jackson—the boy hero of the Waxhaws—is much clearer than the exact location of the village in which he was born.

Settler Andrew Jackson strained himself trying to lift too heavy a load; as a result, Elizabeth Jackson was a widow when her third son was born on March 15, 1767. She named him for his dead father and took refuge with him in the home of her sister, Jane Crawford.

A bright youngster, Andy learned to read at age five. By the time he was eight, he was praised by his schoolmaster as being able to write "a neat, legible hand." One year later, he often served as "public reader," standing on the steps of Captain Crawford's home and reading columns of newspapers aloud to anyone who cared to listen.

The calm and tranquil life of the Waxhaws vanished after July 4, 1776. High excitement prevailed at news that the British had attacked Charles Town. Should they take

Andrew Jackson's birthplace, claimed by both Carolinas.

the city, they'd no doubt move out into the countryside, perhaps as far as the Catawba River.

"We ought to get ready to fight," young Jackson is reputed to have said to friends and relatives.

Words like that from a boy of nine would have been ignored under ordinary circumstances, but Andy was no ordinary boy. Time and again he had demonstrated his willingness to fight fellows twice his weight, usually when taunted about his tendency to drool almost constantly.

In 1776 the boy didn't have to do more than make threatening noises about the British. Repulsed at Charles Town, they did not mount a major offensive in Carolina until 1779.

South Carolina's capital fell on May 12, 1780. Lieutenant Colonel Banastre Tarleton then led his redcoats toward the Back Country. After a long forced march, they clashed with patriots and left the ground covered with the dead. Many wounded were brought to the Waxhaw church, hastily converted into a makeshift hospital.

During weeks of action, the region was sometimes securely held by patriots. At other times it was overrun by the British, who burned crops and houses and destroyed the cattle they did not kill for food.

By 1781 young Andy Jackson was a seasoned member of Crawford's mounted militia. Along with his older brother, the boy was captured in early April, while eating breakfast in the Crawford home.

Redcoats proceeded systematically to smash furniture in the sparsely equipped home. One of their officers, cursing profusely, commanded Andy to clean his boots. The

Upon Andy's refusal, the officer lifted his sword and struck him.

order was instantly refused as being below the dignity of a prisoner of war.

Andrew's brash refusal brought quick reprisal. Lifting his sword, the officer delivered a violent blow aimed directly at the head of his juvenile captive. Throwing up his left arm, Jackson received a cut that left him badly scarred for life, but saved his skull except for a deep gash that reached the bone.

Forced to mount a horse, the bleeding boy was made to guide the British to a nearby home. He, in turn, duped his enemies and managed to warn the man they expected to capture. As punishment, he was forced to march more than forty miles to Camden.

Days later, Elizabeth Jackson rode from the Waxhaws to the prison compound in Camden. Somehow, she persuaded Lord Rowdon to release Andy and his brother Robert, who died two nights after reaching home. Andy became delirious and for hours was at the point of the death.

Gradually recovering, the boy of fourteen made a solemn vow. God being his helper, some day he'd make the British pay for what they had done.

PART THREE:

Red Man/White Man

Osceola. [ENGRAVING AFTER CATLIN PORTRAIT]

16

Flag of Truce Was Osceola's Undoing

"I speak as a friend," General Hernandez began. "What induced you to come?"

He knew the answer to his question. A huge white banner—an impromptu flag of truce—floated above the spot at which whites and Indians were meeting near Fort Peyton, Florida. Each group was nervous and suspicious of the other with good reason. It was now October 27, 1837, and for twenty-three years the Seminole War had been one of America's longest and most deadly conflicts. General Andrew Jackson had crushed Indian forces in 1818; but their strength had grown under the leadership of Osceola, and they had become a serious threat to whites.

Thus the formal parley on a crisp Fall day was significant to leaders of both sides. A working agreement, however tenuous, would save many lives.

Before white men came in sight, Seminole chieftain Osceola had insisted that Coa Hadjo play the role of tribal spokesman. Coa Hadjo pondered Hernandez's opening words, then replied firmly, "We come for good."

Hernandez nodded gravely. But minutes later, without warning, he announced, "I wish all of you [Seminoles] well. But we have been deceived so often that you must come with me. You will get good treatment. You will be glad that you fell into my hands."

Hernandez gave a pre-arranged signal. Before Coa Hadjo, Osceola, and their comrades could seize their loaded guns, forces of Brevet Major James A. Ashby appeared from ambush. Concealed in a thicket on Moultrie Creek, they were within easy gunshot of the Indians who thought they had come to talk peace.

Surgeon Nathan Jarvis, who was present and reported the conversation, watched Osceola closely. He later said that the famous Indian leader showed no sign of surprise.

Resistance would have meant death. Ashby commanded a force of 250 calvarymen and dragoons. The Indians who had a total of just fifty-two rifles, surrendered without firing a shot.

In addition to Osceola and his spokesmen, soldiers that day captured seventy-one warriors and six women. Cavalrymen formed a hollow phalanx. Prodded inside, Indians walked to St. Augustine, where nearly everyone in the town turned out to gape and to cheer.

Osceola wore the bright blue calico shirt and red leggings for which he was noted. Having dressed in order to talk peace, he had a brightly colored shawl over his shoulders and another wrapped around his head.

Gen. Thomas Sidney Jesup, U.S.A., had arranged the plot. Until his death he defended the seizure of Osceola under a flag of truce as "the easiest way to end a bloody business."

As news of the capture spread, many of Jesup's countrymen denounced him. No other incident in the long-drawn struggle between white men and red men quite matches the perfidy of the man then commanding U. S. forces in Florida.

Today as well as a century and a half ago, little is positively known about the early years of Osceola, the most noted Seminole warrior.

Early writers said he was born about 1804, somewhere on the Chattahoochee River. Others insisted he came from "the Tallapoosa River in what is now the state of Georgia." Tribesmen called him As-se-he-ho-lar, or "Black drink," a famous ritual beverage among the Creeks of Georgia and Alabama.

Some whites said that he was the son or grandson of English trader William Powell. Though undocumented, that tradition is so strong that many reports refer to him as Billy Powell.

Known by whatever name, he remained in obscurity until October 1834. He then repudiated an agreement (widely regarded as a sell-out) under which some Seminole leaders had agreed to removal to the west.

Osceola led the famous Christmas massacre of 1835, reputedly as an act of revenge upon whites who had seized his wife as a runaway slave. He and his men fought at Ouithlacoochee, Micanopy, Fort Drane, and many other battlefields.

Following his capture, Osceola was moved to Ft. Moultrie, South Carolina, where he languished in his cell. There he died at age thirty-four. Today the site of his imprisonment is a tourist shrine.

Osceola's captor, Jesup, is now a footnote to history. No one ever painted his portrait; few reference books include his name.

George Catlin's portrait of Osceola hangs in the Smithsonian Institution in Washington, D.C. A national forest, a state park, three counties, twenty towns, two lakes, and two mountains perpetuate the name of the warrior who grieved himself to death in a Carolina prison.

17

Tsali Gave His Life for Fellow Tribesmen

Eastern Cherokees, who were among the most culturally advanced of all native Americans, established themselves as a nation in order to resist the encroachment of whites.

They adopted a constitution, established a capital, and published a newspaper, *The Cherokee Phoenix*. Instead of placating their enemies, these moves made the whites more determined to take over tribal lands.

A few leaders decided that compromise was the lesser of the evils confronting the Cherokees. Hence they signed the Treaty of New Echota, which called for removal of tribesmen to new lands in the West.

Seven million acres "in the Arkansas River region" were to be assigned to deported Indians. Federal authorities agreed to provide two thousand dollars a year for the education of Cherokee children, plus one thousand dollars for purchase of type and a printing press to replace the one destroyed by whites.

Each family moving west of the Great River was to be provided with "a good rifle, a blanket, a kettle, and five pounds of tobacco."

Stockades were built, and Cherokees were herded into them in preparation for the start of removal in June 1838. An estimated 18,000 men, women, and children were ready to begin the march now famous as "The Trail of Tears."

Some of the tribesmen resisted and fled into the wild mountain country of western North Carolina. General

Winfield Scott, who headed U. S. Army units superintending the removal, decided not to pursue fugitives for the moment. He would escort the large contingent of Cherokees to Oklahoma, then send seasoned troops back to flush out the escapees. Scott, who had won national fame by riding into Mexico City as a victor in the Mexican War, was following the orders of Congress, whose decision was strongly advocated by President Andrew Jackson.

Soon after the march began, it became obvious that it would be a debacle. Children, a few women, and occasionally a weak male were unable to stand the pace. Prodded by uniformed soldiers, they staggered forward until

General Winfield Scott. [LIBRARY OF CONGRESS]

they died. At least one Cherokee woman at the limit of her endurance was prodded by a soldier's bayonet.

Furious at the white man's treatment of his wife, Tsali—or Charlie—that night made whispered plans with his relatives in their native language. Sentries on duty heard them speaking but did not understand what was being said.

At dawn Tsali led a suicide squad of young men willing to die to escape to the hills of their birth. In the melee that followed, a soldier was killed.

Tsali, his sons, and other fugitives, joined a band led by Utsala, or Lichen, who had found refuge on the upper Oconaluftee River.

General Winfield Scott believed that the killing of one of his men gave him an opportunity. Instead of waiting, he immediately determined to come to terms with the refugees. Using veteran trader William H. Thomas as a go-between, he made the fugitives an offer.

The Trail of Tears.

If Tsali and his band of escapees would turn themselves in, said Scott, he would permit the remainder of Utsala's followers to remain in the mountains. They could negotiate a settlement with the federal government later.

Comfortably and securely established in a remote cave at the head of Deep Creek, Tsali received word of Thomas's mission and Scott's offer. "I will come in," he said. "I will bring my own. But the rest must be allowed to stay in the mountains."

Speaking for Scott, Thomas gave his solemn word in agreement.

Tsali led the culprits who had reacted to a soldier's brutality: his brother, his oldest son, and two younger sons. Together they marched to the white man's command post and surrendered.

Tradition says that a female missionary, alerted to what was happening, interceded with Army leaders. "Look at Tsali's youngest son," she reputedly urged. "Wasituna (better known to whites as Washington) is only a child. Spare him, in the name of humanity and decency!"

Thus was Wasituna's death sentence commuted, and he survived into the twentieth century. His father, his uncle, and his two older brothers were taken out and shot.

"Tsali did right," Wasituna always said. "He gave himself up and led the others along, for the sake of our people."

As a result of Tsali's sacrifice, eastern Cherokees who had escaped to avoid deportation were permitted to remain in the Great Smokies. Their descendants make up most natives of the Qualla Reservation in western North Carolina.

Unto These Hills, widely believed to be America's most popular outdoor drama, gives a vivid portrayal of the Cherokee Indians' story, including the life—and death—of Tsali.

18

Benjamin Hawkins Smoked the Peace Pipe

"Tustenuggee Thlucco will sign," said the Indian chieftain of mixed blood whom whites knew as Big Warrior. As he stepped forward to make his mark giving consent to the treaty framed by Andrew Jackson, Benjamin Hawkins burst into sobs. Later he explained to his son that "Twenty years of my life were wiped out by a single stroke of a pen."

Commissioners had come together with Indian leaders at Fort Jackson. Hastily erected near the confluence of Alabama's Coosa and Tallapoosa rivers, Fort Jackson was in the heart of Red Stick territory.

Big Warrior, the affluent owner of sixty black slaves, was not there by choice. He and other chiefs invited to the council by Andrew Jackson had been warned that "Destruction will attend a failure to comply."

Numerous Creeks had fought under Jackson at Horseshoe Bend; they came expecting to be rewarded. Many others had been on the side of their own people, loosely allied with the British. Soundly defeated, they came expecting to be punished.

Jackson treated all Creeks alike. Former allies and former enemies were told that they had only hours to decide whether they would cede tribal land to whites or be exiled to the region near Pensacola, Florida.

Since military forces under Jackson had already demonstrated their overwhelming superiority, most Indian leaders—of whom a majority were of mixed blood—followed the lead of Big Warrior. That night they signed away more than half of the Creek domain, an estimated twenty-three million acres. This area included most of present-day Alabama and much of Georgia.

Eyes still moist with tears, Benjamin Hawkins that night resigned as Indian Commissioner for the region south of the Ohio River. He had done all he could to help native Americans, and he had seen years of effort wiped out by a treaty widely described as "unequalled for exorbitance."

Born in Warren County, North Carolina, Hawkins was personally selected by George Washington as an aide. After the Revolution, he became North Carolina's first full-term U. S. Senator.

Partly because he had learned French at the College of New Jersey, Hawkins had been asked to help negotiate several early treaties with Indians. He was so successful in dealing with Cherokees, Choctaws, and Chickasaws that George Washington again appealed to him. This time he wanted Hawkins to become permanent agent for the Creeks. He also was to be superintendent of all Indian tribes south of the Ohio River.

Hawkins' first daughter showed his passionate interest in native Americans. He named her Cherokee.

Hawkins left his Roanoke plantation in November 1796 and entered northwestern South Carolina on the way to his new post. Creek territory was then about four hundred

William McIntosh, field commander of Creeks loyal to Hawkins.

miles from east to west and about two hundred miles from north to south. Hawkins established headquarters near Macon, Georgia, and built a fort named for him; later he moved to a permanent post on the Flint River.

Once firmly established in Creek territory, the ex-senator brought his slaves from Roanoke and used them to teach agriculture to the Indians. He developed a model farm, so large that he often put his brand upon five hundred calves in a single season. Milk was churned by machinery activated by water power.

Tools and implements manufactured at his model plantation were distributed to Creeks and other natives. Those willing to do so could spend weeks on the Flint River model farm, learning how to use tools and to select and plant seeds.

Symbolically "smoking the peace pipe" year after year, Hawkins's dream of reconciliation between red men and white men was shattered in 1811 when the noted orator Tecumseh came to the South. His mission was to enlist as many Indians as possible on the side of the British in the War of 1812.

Hoping to counter the influence of Tecumseh, Benjamin Hawkins organized a regiment of loyal tribesmen. At their head, as commander, he placed half-breed William McIntosh, who was closely related to a governor of Georgia.

McIntosh and his followers fought fiercely against other Creeks in the battle of Horseshoe Bend. Like Hawkins, they felt betrayed when they were given the same treatment as the Red Sticks who had murdered whites at Fort Mims and had opposed Jackson's troops.

Following the debacle at Fort Jackson, Benjamin Hawkins returned to North Carolina after an absence of twenty years. Once more assuming the role of a wealthy and well-educated white man who had experienced political power, he grieved over the treatment given to the Indians he had tried to help. Four years after having been forced to leave the Indians he loved, he died. Until his death he grieved at the wicked ways of his own people.

19

Londoners Gawked When Cherokees Came

Crowds lined the streets of London on June 22, 1730. Many brought food and ale, jostled for positions affording good views, and planned to stay all day, if necessary.

Nearly everyone in the British capital knew that seven genuine Cherokee Indians, all said to be chieftains, were due to pay a second formal visit to King George II.

The chiefs had reached Dover from Charles Town in Carolina aboard the man-o-war *Fox*. Rumor was that something important—perhaps a treaty—was in the making.

Escorted by triumphant Sir Alexander Cumming, the New World natives had been received by the king in the royal chapel at Windsor on June 18. Cumming, who spoke for them and claimed to be a master of their language, had persuaded the ruler to schedule a vivid ceremony as a follow-up to the informal presentation.

Protected by a military escort, Cumming and the Cherokees were forced to move slowly as they approached for the second session with George II. Awestricken Londoners swore that they saw "immense feathers, perhaps of eagles" dangling from the hands of the visitors. That was nothing, compared with the baubles that persons in the know swore to be the scalps of enemies slain in battle. What a place this Carolina must be!

As planned, the Cherokees did present at least five eagle tails and four scalps to the British sovereign. Using

Cunne Shote, one of the Cherokees who went to London in
1762.

German, the only language with which George II was familiar, Sir Alexander asked permission to make a gift of his own.

London newspapers reported with wonder and awe that Cumming explained to the king that while in Appalachie, he had been adopted by the Cherokees. They had named him as their head chief, he said.

Said the *Daily Journal,* "Sir Alexander was in 1730 made lawgiver, commander, leader, and chief of the Cherokee nation at Nequassee in the Cherokee mountains."

As a gesture of fidelity to his own king, "the chief of the Cherokees presented to George II the crown that symbolized his authority over native Americans."

Almost daily from June through October, the *Daily Post* vied with the *Daily Journal* in reporting activities of the Cherokees. Everywhere they went, they were surrounded by crowds and were treated like royalty.

Indians had come to London previously. Sir Walter Raleigh's earliest captains had brought Manteo and Wanchese from Roanoke in 1584. Pocahontas, the exotic New World wife of John Rolfe, had come in 1616. Yet the Cherokees brought from Carolina by Cumming were viewed as somehow different from earlier visitors.

Cumming revealed just how different they were by releasing to newspapers the text of an agreement he reached with the Indians in early October. Native Americans vowed to be perpetual friends of England and to remain loyal to her king!

British authorities later credited the Cumming pact with persuading Cherokees to fight against other Indians and the French in the French and Indian War. In keeping with the spirit of the agreement worked out by Cumming, another group of Carolina natives came to London in 1762. They reaffirmed earlier vows of loyalty and permitted artists to sketch them in all their splendor.

This time, however, the visit turned sour. Someone, perhaps a secret agent in the pay of the French, poisoned the interpreter. Able to communicate only in the most halting fashion, the Cherokees were sent home with no announcement of the type of treaty made in 1730.

Until the outbreak of the American Revolution and the subsequent upheaval in trans-Atlantic shipping, Cherokees came to England at intervals. However, none of them excited the wonder tinged with fear evoked by Sir Alexander Cumming's scalp- and feather-laden chieftains.

Cherokees who went to London in 1762. [BUREAU OF AMERICAN ETHNOLOGY]

PART FOUR:

The Long Fight for Freedom

Colonel William Moultrie, later made a general.

20

William Moultrie Was First to Fight the British

Major General Charles Lee, immaculate in his elaborate uniform, looked down his nose at ragtag Col. William Moultrie. "You will dismantle this slaughter pen at once," he ordered. "Take your men into Charleston and wait for further orders."

Whistling to his ever-present dogs, the man who despised George Washington, but who was his second in command, climbed on his horse and headed back to Virginia.

Charleston-born Moultrie ignored the orders of his commander. Having personally selected Sullivan's Island, he knew it was the best place at which to place guns to stop the big British ships that were sure to come, sooner or later.

Men of his Second Carolina Regiment had cut palmetto trees, notched their ends, and fastened them together to form a tall rampart. Behind this makeshift barrier, they placed sixteen feet of beach sand.

Any military engineer could have taken one look at Fort Sullivan and known that it was the work of an amateur. General Lee was no amateur. He wanted the place abandoned, but he didn't remain to see his orders carried out. He believed that though the South was important, the real action in the coming American Revolution would be far to the north.

British leaders had other ideas.

They knew that while Charleston wasn't as important as New York, Philadelphia, and Boston, it was the colonies' major import–export center south of Norfolk. Furthermore, its deep, broad harbor was ideal for the British gunboats that sailed up and down the American seacoast.

June 26, 1776, saw Britain's first move toward armed invasion of the emerging United States. Two ships of the line, plus six frigates, mounted 230 guns and carried eight regiments of infantry under the command of Lord Cornwallis. They were sighted on the horizon, headed directly for Charleston.

William Moultrie had thirty-one guns and 400 men, plus palmetto logs and sand. The outcome of the impending battle was clear to everyone except Moultrie and a few subordinates such as Francis Marion. These patriots refused to admit the possibility of defeat.

Under plans developed by Cornwallis and General Sir Henry Clinton, the invaders would make a two-pronged attack. With guns blazing, ships anchored in the harbor would destroy the Americans' fortifications. Simultaneously, regiments of infantry would use small boats to seize positions in the rear and make it impossible for the defeated patriots to retreat.

June 28, 1776, saw the twenty-eight-gun *Actaeon* drop anchor at its preassigned position. Close behind her was the stately *Bristol,* a ship-of-the-line with fifty great naval guns. Next came the *Experiment* with another fifty guns, followed by the twenty-eight-gun frigates *Solebay, Sphinx, Syren,* and *Friendship.*

When vessels manned by invaders had taken their positions, they let loose a nearly simultaneous blast such as North America had never before heard. Under cover of the noise and smoke, small boats filled with redcoats headed for inlets that would take them behind Fort Sullivan.

Surveying the tiny fortification through a glass, Clinton could not believe what he saw. His expert gunners had hit their mark many times in the first volley, but the soft palmetto logs cushioned by sand appeared to be undamaged.

Moultrie's men began firing their smaller guns, not in volleys but one by one. A lucky shot cut the anchor cable of the *Bristol,* causing the huge vessel suddenly to yaw and shift out of line with the tide. That left the stern of the British ship within easy range of American gunners.

Soon the mainmast of the *Bristol* fell; her mizzenmast followed a few minutes later. Drifting, the stricken vessel diverted frigates from their courses, and three of them became entangled. While sailors tried to free tangled lines, American fire cut the *Actaeon* to pieces. Drifting out of control, the ship ran aground at a spot that later became the site of a U. S. military installation, Fort Sumter.

Pounded by heavy guns from time to time during a ten-hour fight, the palmetto fort that the military expert from the North believed to be "a slaughter pen" stood firm. One by one, the British ships still under sail withdrew. When night fell, sailors and soldiers from the stranded *Actaeon* rowed out to sea, where they were picked up and taken aboard other vessels.

Francis Marion, who had fired the last shot of the battle, directed his gun toward the immense *Bristol*. Two officers and three seamen were cut down, and a cabin was smashed. British observers did not know that their foes had run out of powder, and would be unable to fire again.

After the invading flotilla retreated, Americans boarded the stranded *Actaeon* and seized her bell as a prize before setting her afire. William Moultrie, a mere colonel of a colonial regiment, had turned back the first British attempt at armed invasion of territory destined to become part of the United States.

Grateful South Carolinians renamed Fort Sullivan in his honor. Years later, Fort Moultrie was the prison in which the Indian chief Osceola grieved—or starved—himself to death after being seized under a flag of truce. It was at Fort Moultrie that Edgar Allan Poe conceived and wrote "The Gold Bug."

The finest tribute paid to the first American to defeat the British is symbolic. South Carolina's state seal depicts a sturdy palmetto tree that proudly surmounts an uprooted oak. Warships fashioned from oak logs were turned back by a "hopelessly out-gunned and out-manned regiment of South Carolina amateurs."

21

Penelope Barker Led Nation's First Women's Protest

"It is time for women to act. We must show the men that we are to be reckoned with," Penelope Barker insisted repeatedly in 1774.

Tradition credits her with having gone from house to house in Edenton, the capital of Carolina for forty years. Some friends were easily persuaded to back her scheme. Others held back at first, but yielded under her prodding.

October 25, 1774, saw Penelope and her friends converge upon the home of Mrs. Elizabeth King. There they held the nation's first women's protest meeting. Many had come from outlying counties.

"We cannot be indifferent," began a brief open letter written that day. Stressing the importance of the public good, the document ended with a veiled threat: "we do therefore accordingly subscribe to this paper, as a witness of our fixed intention and solemn determination."

Abigail Charlton was the first to affix her signature, and Penelope Barker added hers halfway down the first of two long columns. By the time the second column was filled, fifty-one women had gone on record as being unwilling to "conform to that pernicious custom of drinking tea."

What's more, they launched what may have been the earliest of all "Buy American" movements. They solemnly vowed not to buy clothing or other merchandise manufactured in England.

Men with hatchets staged the Boston Tea Party in December 1773. Aboard the ship *Dartmouth*, they broke

Unexpurgated version of the "Edenton Tea Party." [North Carolina Department of Archives and History]

open 342 chests of English tea and dumped leaves into the harbor.

Events on that dramatic day are remembered everywhere. Not so familiar is the fact that taxed tea went to three additional ports. Charles Town, South Carolina, southernmost point at which taxed tea entered the British colonies, saw docking of the tea ship *London* on December 22, 1773.

Patriots refused to pay duties imposed by Parliament. Three pence per pound seemed small, until it was realized that the British East India Company planned to pump 600,000 pounds of tea into the colonies in one year.

Most Americans, including the ladies in and around Edenton, knew that even with tax added, tea was a bargain. Untaxed tea was more expensive in Britain than the taxed tea being sent to America by the boatload.

Leaders of the British East India Company were sure

that their American market would grow by leaps and bounds. Edenton ladies showed that bewigged males sitting in a London board room could be woefully mistaken. They pledged themselves not to use tea because they opposed the tax, not the price.

Word of actions by female activists spread rapidly. Along the entire Atlantic Seaboard, tea became the focus of colonial protest.

Britain responded by imposing a large fine upon Boston. It was deliberately made large enough to cover the entire cost of tea dumped into the harbor; so the net effect of the Boston Tea Party upon the colonial balance sheet was negative.

Not so in the South.

Inspired by the ladies of Edenton, Carolinians by the hundreds swore off tea for the duration. So did many in still thinly populated Georgia. With tea not selling, many casks of it remained in the Charleston warehouses for months.

As the Revolution broke out and the patriots eventually gained control of Charleston, they seized the stored tea. Selling it tax free, they quickly sold the entire shipment. Ironically, the same tea upon which the colonists were unwilling to pay a tax to Britain was used to help finance the war!

British artist Philip Dawe is believed to have created the early caricature of "A Society of Patriotic Ladies at Edenton in North Carolina" that circulated in London some time in 1775. In it he included a dog urinating on a chest of British tea. Though he included the dog in order to poke fun at American women, not all viewers were amused. A later artist placed the dog in a sleeping position with its head on the lap of a sitting child.

There is no certainty that Penelope Barker ever saw either version of the sketch that mocked the actions of the women she led. Were she alive today and given her choice, there's little doubt about which artist's conception she would endorse. "That dog is giving British tea exactly what it deserves," she'd surely say.

22

Nathanael Greene Outfoxed the British

"Matters are going from bad to worse in the South," said George Washington. "As things stand, the Carolinas may well hold the key to the outcome."

General Nathanael Greene, age thirty-eight, eyed his commander-in-chief with eager expectation. Sensitive to Washington's unwillingness to be interrupted, he said nothing.

"I need you badly here," continued Washington, "but the South needs you even more. You will find yourself outmanned and heavily outgunned. Your sole chance of victory will be use of superior strategy.

"Though you know little of the region, you will learn quickly," he added and paused for a reply.

"When do I leave, sir?" was Greene's terse acceptance of the reassignment.

Headed toward Charlotte, North Carolina, the veteran of Trenton, Brandywine, Valley Forge, and Monmouth made crude but workable maps of the regions through which he passed. At every opportunity the New Jersey native asked old-timers about rivers, snow, and spring rains.

Horatio Gates relinquished command to Greene on December 4, 1780. Immediately Greene began giving orders aimed at implementing the plan he had developed during the long journey south.

He realized it would be suicide to meet Cornwallis and his veterans in open battle, but perhaps he could draw them out of their entrenched positions. To accomplish this, Greene executed one of the most spectacular retreats

*General Nathanael
Greene.* [Nineteenth
century woodcut]

in military history.

Racing against time in a bid to stay ahead of spring rains, he and his men forded the Catawba River at Trading Ford. Before the redcoats could follow, the Catawba became impassable. By the time they resumed the chase, the patriots were north of Virginia's Dan River.

Cornwallis found the Dan so high and turbulent that he gave up chase and returned to North Carolina. He made his headquarters at Hillsboro.

Greene pored over maps and talked endlessly with local woodsmen and guides. After careful deliberation, he picked Guilford Court House, about five miles from Greensboro, as a site at which he would have a fighting chance.

Most of his troops were raw militiamen who had never faced gunfire. That gave Greene about 900 veterans against the 2,213 trained troops Cornwallis had brought from Europe.

In preparing for battle, Greene established a line of militia in an open field, with a second line of inexperienced men in a wood about three hundred yards behind them. He put his small contingent of regulars on a hill near the courthouse, another four hundred yards to the rear.

As expected, the British easily routed the first line of defense. Sheltered by trees, the second line held and delivered withering fire at Cornwallis's troops. While their foes wavered, veterans of the First Maryland moved forward with bayonets and charged.

In desperation, Cornwallis ordered his ranks to open, then fired his large cannons through the hole at the Marylanders. Having checked the patriots, the British moved forward. They carried the hill and repulsed every assault wave directed against it.

As evening approached, Greene withdrew. Since all the horses used to pull the pieces were dead or wounded, he left his artillery on the field. By textbook standards, it was a clear victory for Cornwallis.

But Greene counted only 79 killed and 184 wounded. Cornwallis lost 93 killed, 413 wounded, and 26 missing, a

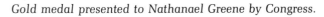

Gold medal presented to Nathanael Greene by Congress.

total of about one-fourth of his entire force.

In due time, Parliament received a formal report of the victory at Guilford Court House. Charles James Fox wryly observed to fellow lawmakers that "another such victory would destroy the British Army in the colonies."

With British domination of North Carolina ended, Greene took his hungry, half-naked men south. On September 8, 1781, they won a spectacular victory at Eutaw Springs, South Carolina. Redcoats retreated into fortified positions in Charles Town; Congress voted a special gold medal for Greene.

Though the enemy held the capital of the colony, Greene sent agents there. Under the noses of the British in Charles Town, they purchased wagonload after wagonload of desperately needed clothing and supplies.

Having little or no money, Greene gave his own promissory notes to Charles Town merchants. Learning that Washington had trapped Cornwallis at Yorktown, he exulted, "We have been beating the bush, and the General has come to catch the bird!"

Second only to Washington in importance as a Revolutionary commander, Greene was deeply in debt at the end of the war. He owed nine thousand pounds for clothing, salt, hospital supplies, and ammunition bought in Charles Town.

Grateful lawmakers of South Carolina and Georgia gave him money and land, but not enough money and perhaps too much land. He died, impoverished, at his Mulberry Grove plantation in Georgia at age forty-four.

It was there that his widow played hostess to would-be school teacher Eli Whitney who invented the cotton gin while a guest at the plantation of the Rhode Islander who had outfoxed the British.

23

Sharpshooter Who Spared George Washington Lies At Kings Mountain

London's public record office holds the handwritten original of an amazing document. Had it not been preserved, the story of Patrick Ferguson's sighting of George Washington would be dismissed as a myth.

According to researchers, records indicate that the commander-in-chief of still-raw recruits went on reconnaissance on September 7, 1776, to discover whether colonial units at Chad's Ford on Brandywine Creek might be able to stop the British troops that were camped just four miles from the ford.

At the same time, three British soldiers were on patrol far ahead of their own lines. One of them, Major Patrick Ferguson, was a famous sharpshooter and inventor of a light breechloading rifle. Once, while demonstrating his weapon for King George III, he had hit the bull's-eye at one hundred yards, while lying flat on his back.

According to Ferguson's written account, he spotted two American riders. One of them wore "a remarkably large cocked hat."

First he signaled to his men that the foes were to be shot as soon as they came in range. Then suddenly he reversed his orders, stepped out into view, and shouted a demand for surrender. The rider in the big cocked hat wheeled his horse and raced for cover.

"I could have lodged half a dozen of balls in him," Ferguson wrote, "but it was not pleasant to fire at a man's back, so I let him alone."

George Washington, who didn't realize the extent of the danger, rode back to his camp. After fighting in several engagements, Patrick Ferguson was given temporary rank of colonel and sent south at the head of a band of sharpshooters.

In North Carolina the man who might have altered the course of the American Revolution by one squeeze of his trigger finger decided it was time "to fight Americans with Americans." He issued a call for all Tories, or Loyalists, to get their rifles and join his forces. Three years to the day after his failure to shoot George Washington, he led about 1,100 American Tories in North Carolina against "backwater men, a set of mongrels," known to be getting ready to meet him in battle.

Col. Isaac Shelby had assembled one band in Sullivan County, North Carolina, Col. John Sevier headed others who came from what was then Washington County, North Carolina. About 1,100 patriots were ready to risk their lives in combat with at least 1,700 Tories.

"Nolichucky Jack" Sevier persuaded fellow leaders to pick 900 men with the best horses. Most had Deckhard rifles; all carried bags of parched corn.

These experienced frontiersmen moved slowly up the slope of the long, rugged hill called Kings Mountain. Soon they tethered their horses and proceeded upward, always under cover of bushes and shrubs. During the battle, the Tories had no targets except for brief flashes of gunfire. Trapped at the crest of Kings Mountain, they were so exposed that foes called them "sitting ducks."

The Watauga men and their comrades showed none of the compassion and sportsman-like behavior Patrick Ferguson exhibited three years earlier. They mowed down their Tory foes without mercy.

Patrick Ferguson took at least three balls; when he fell, Col. William Campbell roared to Americans who were killing fellow countrymen almost indiscriminately, "For God's sake, quit! It's murder to shoot now!"

The Tories' defeat was complete; nearly the entire army

was killed, wounded, or captured, while the patriots lost twenty-eight killed, plus sixty-two wounded.

Though the forces involved were small, the impact of Kings Mountain was large. While sending the British reeling in defeat, it boosted the morale of patriots everywhere.

*   *   *

Partly because it was the site of one of the decisive battles of the Revolution, Kings Mountain was made into one of our largest military parks. Great oaks and pines cover much of its 3,950 acres. Park personnel gladly point out one vast poplar that "maybe was a sapling at the time of the battle." Except for the rock cairn that marks the last resting place of the sharpshooter who spared Washington, there is little to indicate that the fate of America was once in the balance here.

Kings Mountain National Military Park lies in South Carolina, just below the North Carolina line. Only three miles off Interstate 85, it is open every day but Christmas and New Year's.

24

Sergeant Jasper Saved the Flag!

Big naval guns fired from British warships threatened to destroy Fort Sullivan in Charleston harbor. Crowds of civilians watched the action from the city's famous seaside Battery.

"They were looking on with anxious fears and hopes," according to William Moultrie, commander of the patriots.

Some had their fathers, brothers, and husbands in the battle. Their hearts must have been pierced at every broadside.

After some time, our flag was shot away. Their hopes were then gone, and they gave up all for lost! They supposed that we had struck our flag and had given up the fort.

Perceiving that the flag was shot away and had fallen outside the fort, Sergeant Jasper jumped from one of the embrasures. He brought the flag up through a heavy fire, fixed it upon a spunge-staff [used by artillerymen] and planted it upon the ramparts again.

Our flag once more waving in the air revived the drooping spirits of our men. They then resisted so valiantly that the British gave up and retired to deep water.

Nearly forgotten today, except for his impact upon the map, Sergeant Jasper was once the most noted southern hero of the American Revolution. His exploit at Charleston, almost duplicated later at Savannah, made his name a household word: "*Sergeant Jasper rescued the flag!*"

When that message was relayed through the countryside by word of mouth, patriots of 1776 reacted much as Americans did following the raising of the flag on Iwo Jima during World War II.

Southerners named eight counties and at least twenty-two towns and villages in honor of the man who saved the flag. Hundreds of families bestowed the name Jasper upon sons on whom they had high hopes.

Strangely, the record suggests that the man who won fame as a member of a South Carolina regiment was neither an American by birth nor a patriot by choice. Late in October 1767, ninety immigrants took the oath of allegiance to Britain, not to one of her already rebellious colonies, at the Philadelphia office of Thomas Willing, Esq. One who was unable to sign his own name on the register was listed as John William Jasper.

Believed to have been born and reared in Germany and named Johann Wilhelm by his parents, the youthful immigrant didn't find in Philadelphia the opportunities he was seeking. It is believed that Jasper then settled in Georgia. Although land was cheap there, he was unable to send for his sweetheart in Philadelphia for lack of money. Thus at about age twenty-five he enlisted in a South Carolina regiment, not for love of America but because he would be paid in cash.

"Sergeant Jasper saved the flag." [Eighteenth century woodcut]

Small as it was, Jasper's pay enabled him to bring his sweetheart to Charleston. They married there and became parents of twins.

Soon after the twins were born, the British picked Charleston as a major target. It was during the ensuing battle that the German who fought for pay captured the imagination of all who saw him in action and all who heard about it.

South Carolina Governor Rutledge presented Jasper with a sword and offered him a commission. He accepted the weapon but turned down the promotion. A man who could not read and write had no business being an officer, he said.

Universally known simply as Sergeant Jasper, he moved with his unit into the region of Savannah. Legend says that a certain Jones, a handcuffed prisoner of the British, was due to be taken to Savannah to be hanged. With a few comrades Sergeant Jasper got the drop on a band of eight heavily armed British. Forced to surrender their weapons and their prisoner, the redcoats were themselves placed in irons and taken to a nearby American camp.

Days later, on October 9, 1779, when patriots decided they must take Savannah from the British at whatever cost, Jasper was again in the front line of action with the flag in his hands. This time his mission was to plant the colors of the Second South Carolina Infantry upon a redoubt at Spring Hill. He received a direct hit and fell dead, still gripping the pole of the flag.

A redoubt at Fort Moultrie was soon named Jasper Battery in his honor, and Savannah erected a splendid bronze monument to him. Throughout the South political leaders moved to make his name immortal by voting to bestow it upon villages, towns, and counties.

Except for George Washington, Benjamin Franklin, and the Marquis de LaFayette, no Revolutionary leader's name appears on the map of the South more frequently than does that of the illiterate German mercenary who twice offered his life for a flag.

25

Dan Morgan Masterminded "Most Imitated Battle"

"Remember, boys, three shots is all I ask!" Wincing from rheumatism, buckskin-clad Dan Morgan wore no insignia of rank. Members of his militia companies regarded him almost as one of them. Even though he had been a brigadier general for a few months, his attitude hadn't changed at all.

Using his lungs as though he were bellowing at men and horses during his years as a wagon master, Morgan shouted assurances to the militiamen. "You will win! Follow my orders exactly! You'll see the enemy run! Get ready, boys, they're on the way!"

Morgan had taken part in the expedition against Canada and in the bloody Saratoga campaign. Still, he was untried as a commanding officer.

Gen. Nathanael Greene, defeated by the British at Camden, was in trouble; and George Washington sent Morgan to his aid. Badly outnumbered, the patriots split their force. Pursued by Cornwallis—perhaps the finest professional soldier of the Revolution—Greene retreated into North Carolina.

Morgan's small band was being hunted by the elite corps headed by Col. Banastre Tarleton, all seasoned regulars. They knew that most of Morgan's men were hastily summoned militia with no battle experience and little stomach to get it. Men of this sort had been known to turn tail and run when confronted by booming artillery and flashing sabers.

George Washington (center) congratulates Morgan.

To the bewilderment of his subordinates, Dan Morgan picked a field and deliberately waited for Tarleton and his men to mount an attack. From a boy of nine who'd taken one of his father's old bulls into the British camp and sold it, he learned that enemies were close on his heels. They would catch up soon, no matter what he did. His only chance was to have a meeting ground of his choice, plus unconventional deployment of his forces.

Hannah's Cowpens, named for a man who once grazed a herd of cattle at the site, was a rolling slope topped by two small hills. To the rear was Broad River, which was too turbulent to be crossed and effectively cut off retreat.

"Remember Tarleton's Quarter!" Morgan shouted again and again as he rode along his lines early on January 17, 1781.

His message—actually a warning—required no explanation. It was well known that Colonel Tarleton was so disdainful of patriots that he had more than once refused to take prisoners. Men who had thrown down their weapons and surrendered had been cut down by the sword blades of Tarleton's redcoats.

Although Dan Morgan didn't say it, his message to his inexperienced men was clear: "With the river behind you,

you have two choices. You can fight like veterans and whip the British here, or you can die in these Cowpens."

Ignoring tried and tested strategy by which men facing attack always put their finest troops in the forefront, Morgan deliberately stationed his militia where they'd meet the first wave of assault. Behind them he placed a second line of troops made up of Continental soldiers, plus a small force of mounted dragoons.

Members of his militia company understood that once every man had fired three of the twelve rounds he carried, the entire body was to make an orderly withdrawal. Continentals knew they were expected to hold their positions regardless of what happened.

British scouts described for Tarleton the unusual spot at which the colonists were deployed. Delighted at the ignorance of the American commander who'd placed his forces in such fashion, the redcoat leader sent his little three-pound cannon (commonly called "grasshoppers") forward.

One volley from the grasshoppers should have dispersed the untrained men in Morgan's front ranks. Incredibly, they stood their ground. It was too late for Tarleton to change his tactics; his battleline was already moving forward.

Though they had no combat experience, many of the militia were skilled hunters. They used their weapons so effectively the British advance faltered, then halted. As ordered, the first line of patriots made an orderly retreat to the rear.

The British regrouped. Tarleton threw in the seventy-first Highlanders—his last fresh troops—in a frantic bid to take the hill held by Continentals. Repulsed, they swirled around in confusion.

Precisely at this point, Morgan did what no other commander had done. He sent his militia back into the fray. Having nearly circled the American position, they struck the British left rear. Simultaneously, Morgan's dragoons hit the British right.

Redcoats began surrendering. Jubilant patriots yelled

"Tarleton's quarter!" and prepared to cut them down. Their commander intervened, but not before 39 British officers and 61 enlisted men lay dead on the field. More than 200 of the enemy had been wounded; about 600 were taken prisoner. Patriots had lost 12 men and counted less than 60 wounded.

Military strategists who learned of what had happened in northwestern South Carolina at first refused to believe the news. When fresh reports made it impossible to deny, many dubbed the battle of Cowpens as "the most extraordinary event of the American conflict."

Nathanael Greene received from Morgan a firsthand account of tactics used. Later, at least twice, Greene would employ the same strategy against numerically superior forces. Again in the War of 1812 "Morgan's battle plan" was used so effectively that Cowpens became famous as the most imitated battle of the American Revolution.

One-time wagon master Morgan had done what everyone thought impossible. He had used raw recruits to turn the tide against battle-tested veterans!

General Dan Morgan, dressed much more elegantly than usual.

26

Elijah Clarke Was Rewarded for His Heroism

Hannah Clarke made no secret of her discontent with Edgecombe County, North Carolina. Her husband and sons worked from sunup to sundown, but they were unable to scratch a good living out of the worn-out soil. Game was becoming so scarce that the only way to put meat on the table was to butcher a pig or a calf.

Initially by word of mouth, and then from a newspaper in tatters from much handling, Hannah heard that good land was cheap in the West. "Go and see for yourself," she urged her husband, Elijah.

Too much of a backwoodsman even to try to find a job in Rocky Mount, Elijah didn't take much persuasion. He made a foray west of the Holston River, but much of the rocky land in present-day eastern Tennessee looked as bad or worse than his own.

Back home, he told his wife and sons, "Things don't look so good over there. Let's try the South."

Having no firsthand knowledge of the region, they headed toward the coast. It took only a few weeks in Craven County for them to realize they couldn't make a living there. So they left for the southwestern frontier, Georgia's Indian country.

By the time they settled northwest of Augusta, Georgia, Elijah was forty years old, past his prime and well aware of it. Still, he was making good progress at clearing land for a fine farm when the British began making raids throughout the region.

Many settlers fled. Others, including Clarke, sent their

Elijah Clarke, as portrayed by an artist who never saw him.

wives to South Carolina for what they considered to be safety. Since Elijah's neighbors had elected him captain of a little band of volunteer rangers, he and his men stayed behind to fight the redcoats and their Indian allies.

When enemies burned his house, Clarke became fighting mad. He raised a regiment and marched at the head of it as colonel, in spite of the fact that he'd had little or no schooling.

"Boys," he said one day after poring over crude maps, "let's go run the redcoats out of Augusta. As long as they have it, they control most of the Savannah River."

Poorly planned and launched by inexperienced men, the assault upon Fort Cornwallis in Augusta was futile. Clarke lost over half of his men, more by desertion than from British bullets.

Retreating into South Carolina, the remnant was pursued by a band of Tories and Indians that soon was joined by Patrick Ferguson, one of Britain's finest professional soldiers, who took command and continued the chase.

By now reduced to a handful of woodsmen, Clarke's group found they could easily elude the enemy. Hence they led Ferguson and his men through swamps and woods until they gave up in exhaustion. It was this foray after Clarke and his men that led to Ferguson's defeat and death at Kings Mountain.

As for Clarke, he had had enough of ordinary civilians turned soldiers. Knowing he couldn't win a command in the Continental forces, he went back to western North Carolina and present-day Tennessee and recruited over-the-mountain men to augment his force.

Artists of a later era have depicted Elijah Clarke as though he were a Virginia gentleman, but he probably looked much like the barefooted, skin-clan riflemen he led.

Still fuming at his defeat at Augusta, he returned there aided by Henry ("Light Horse Harry") Lee. There the Americans stormed the fortress and seized it as an outpost for the patriots.

Terse accounts of the siege of Augusta suggest that the victors showed the defeated enemy no quarter. Clarke and his men remembered what the British had done earlier. Finding armed patriots out of their reach, "Tories and Indians fell on old men, children, and women. Lads were obliged to dance naked between two large fires until they were scorched to death. Men were scalped and cut to pieces; then the pieces were hung up."

During the three-week siege, 23 Americans were killed outright or received mortal wounds. Another 35 were wounded by British bullets. But the British counted 52 deaths, plus 354 additional casualties; only a few escaped without a wound. Men who looked as though they were on a bear hunt had overcome Britain's finest regular soldiers.

Following the surrender of the British high command at Yorktown, grateful Southern colonies rewarded many heroes of the Revolution. Georgia "made Col. Clarke a Compliment of the Plantation of Thomas Waters," a Tory whose land had been seized. Years later, Georgia lawmakers honored the self-taught frontiersman by creating Clarke County, site of the University of Georgia.

However, it was his home state, North Carolina, that really most rewarded the man who, like many Revolutionary soldiers, was pauperized at the end of the struggle. Well aware that the man from Edgecombe had led his men into battle only in Georgia and South Carolina, the North Carolina legislature voted him a purse of $30,444.

Records are scattered and incomplete, so it is impossible to draw absolute conclusions. Nevertheless all the evidence suggests that the Tar Heel who could barely scribble reports to his superiors received the biggest cash reward, or bonus, of any Revolutionary leader.

PART FIVE:

Our So Un-Civil War

General Joseph E. Johnston.

General William T. Sherman.

27

Sherman's Plan Would Have Avoided Reconstruction

"The mass of the people south will never trouble us again, Ellen," wrote Gen. William T. Sherman to his wife. "They have suffered terribly, and I now feel disposed to befriend them."

Posted from Raleigh in April 1865, that little-known personal letter reveals the Sherman whom few people in the North or the South know.

Most Americans remember Sherman for his infamous "march to the sea." Nearly forgotten are events that took place near Durham.

Joseph E. Johnston commanded the Confederate Army of Tennessee in 1865. The last major fighting force of the Rebels, it had moved into North Carolina to evade Union armies.

However, the Federals moved too rapidly to give Johnston a breather. Weighing his options, he decided to seek the best terms he could get. At his headquarters he drafted, then revised, a letter.

The Confederate leader's document was hand-delivered to William T. Sherman on April 14. It requested an armistice for the benefit of both armies and ended with a short but vital question, "What are the best terms upon which I may surrender my army?"

Sherman and Johnston met under a flag of truce at noon on April 17 in the yard of the James Bennett place, about two miles from Durham Station. After two hours, they came to a general agreement. Johnston would disband the last effective fighting force of the Confederacy. He also

113

would order Rebels in Alabama, Mississippi, Louisiana, and Texas to lay down their weapons. In return, Sherman drafted terms designed to create an honorable peace and a swift return of seceded states to the Union.

All fighting men of the rank of colonel or below would be pardoned upon taking an oath of allegiance to the United States. Every soldier who would return home, observe his parole, and obey the laws "would be entirely free from disturbance by U. S. authority."

Southern legislatures would remain intact. Elected officials would keep control of weapons held in their own armories. Every Southerner ready to submit to the authority of the U. S. Constitution would "regain his position as a citizen, free and equal in all respects." Incredibly, Sherman even promised that citizens could sue the Federal government for the value of freed slaves.

Sherman had offered far more than Joe Johnston had dared to expect or hope. With spirits soaring to the point of ecstasy, he ordered his men to surrender their weapons. Every available building was soon filled with rifles, sabers, and pistols.

Meanwhile, Secretary of War Edwin M. Stanton, who had already shown himself to be an implacable foe of the South, now demanded that North Carolina native Andrew Johnston, successor to assassinated Abraham Lincoln, convene his cabinet at once. Their session started at 8:00 P.M. on April 21, only hours after Sherman's telegram was received from Raleigh.

Following a marathon cabinet meeting, Sherman was ordered to resume fighting. Each of his top subordinates received a telegram instructing him to disregard any and all promises of peace. Gen. U. S. Grant was ordered to relieve Sherman of command, and Sherman was ordered to report to Washington at once for interrogation.

Opponents of "an easy peace" grilled Sherman minutely, then reprimanded him. To his face some of them called him a lunatic and a traitor.

"To say that I was merely angry would hardly express the state of my feelings," Sherman wrote to Ellen. "I was outraged beyond measure."

Having repudiated the Sherman–Johnston pact, Stanton of Ohio—Sherman's native state—led a group of Congressmen in shaping harsh new terms for the stricken South.

Some of the effects were felt at once.

On learning that the armies had laid down their weapons, Zebulon Vance went to Greensboro to surrender to Gen. John M. Schofield. Schofield refused to make him a prisoner and told him to go home.

Therefore Vance put his saddle horses and two mules in a freight car and went home to Statesville. Once Stanton's terms superseded Sherman's, Vance was arrested at his home and shipped to Old Capitol Prison in Washington. His experience was indicative of the military occupation and repressive Reconstruction era that followed.

Had Sherman's generous terms not been rejected out of hand, the South would have been spared Reconstruction. Because he was a popular commander, his peace plan would have had a fighting chance for success if Stanton and his allies had not prevented its implementation.

Sherman had been in long conferences with Lincoln and was confident that the peace he made with Johnston reflected the president's views. But Abraham Lincoln was mortally wounded on April 14, the same day Sherman received Johnston's overture for peace. In the emotional climate that followed the assassination, Sherman's plan for an honorable peace and healing of the wounds between North and South was doomed.

28

Gunmaker Said He'd Put an End to War

"I witnessed almost daily the departure of troops to the front and the return of the wounded, sick, and dead," said Richard J. Gatling in describing the origin of the gun upon which his name was bestowed.

"It occurred to me that if I could invent a machine—a gun—which by its rapidity of fire could enable one man to do as much battle duty as a hundred, that it would eliminate the necessity for large armies.

"Such a gun would reduce exposure to battle and disease, and would become a great life-saving device."

Writing to Miss Lizzie Jarvis, that's how Richard Jordan Gatling, M.D., explained his invention of a rapid-fire gun.

Born in Hertford County, North Carolina, Gatling began tinkering with machinery as a small boy. As an adolescent, he helped his father perfect a cottonseed sowing machine. His experience on Jordan Gatling's prosperous farm launched him on a lifelong search—frequently successful—for better and faster machinery that could do work formerly performed by hand.

Richard worked with his father on a machine for thinning cotton plants. Then he taught school for a year and at age twenty opened a country store. His business venture lasted only a few months because his fascination with machinery led him to devote most of his time to the invention of a screw propeller.

Next came a rice sowing machine that was so successful he won a patent and attracted the interest of financial backers. Since Carolina had no facilities for mass production of his rice-sower, he went to St. Louis and then to Indianapolis and Philadelphia in search of a manufacturer.

Icebound on a river steamer during the winter of 1845, Gatling came down with smallpox and found that there was no physician on the boat. Ever busy, he enrolled in the Medical College of Ohio in Cincinnati to study medicine so he could take care of himself and members of his family. Though he never practiced medicine, for the remainder of his life he was addressed as Dr. Gatling.

Prior to the Civil War, Gatling invented a hemp braking machine and a steam plow. With the outbreak of war, he turned his mind toward military machines and invented a steam ram for naval use.

On November 4, 1862, Gatling won patent #36,836 for a rapid-fire gun. Six rifled barrels, each equipped with a striker, revolved around a hand-powered central axis. Charges fed from a hopper by gravity.

Two men were required to operate the gun, which was first produced in Indianapolis. Explaining his invention, the man trained to save lives by medicine said, "I made inquiry at the depot, and found that out of eighteen dead, only three or four had been killed by bullets. The rest died in hospitals from disease.

Dr. Richard J. Gatling.
[DICTIONARY OF
AMERICAN PORTRAITS]

"Out of my own experience, I knew that it was possible to sow seeds in a scientific way by machinery. Why not shoot by machinery—and have one man do the work of one hundred, leaving the other ninety-nine at home?"

At maximum efficiency, Gatling's original gun sprayed out about two hundred bullets per minute. Nothing remotely like it had ever been seen on a battlefield; yet top officials in Washington showed little interest.

Gen. Benjamin F. Butler bought twelve guns without authorization from higher authorities. Fighting men used these $1,000-weapons in the James River campaign of May and June 1864.

Gatling's guns performed so well that official Washington sat up and took notice. Leaders decided to adopt his invention; but by the time orders were placed and manufacture was under way, Lee and Grant had met at Appomattox, Virginia, and the war was over.

An improved 1865 model with ten barrels raised firepower to three hundred shots per minute. Gatling still was not satisfied. By 1898 his latest model—already called a gat—had a battery-operated motor. It could shoot at the rate of three thousand rounds per minute.

Heralded as a substitute for troops, the gun devised by the inventor who had started with farm machinery attracted the interest of Napoleon III and other European leaders. Gatling, who seemed to have forgotten his claim to have devised the rapid-fire weapon to put an end to war, demonstrated it in many parts of the world.

The Gatling gun played decisive roles in the Spanish–American, the Franco–Prussian, and the Russo–Japanese wars, as well as dozens of smaller conflicts. For the British Empire at its zenith, it was the device for keeping restless colonials at bay throughout the world.

If the machinery-minded son of a Maney's Neck planter ever had misgivings about being a weapons inventor, he said nothing. Ironically he became wealthy from a gun that magnified war's horror instead of reducing it.

29

Showdown in Charleston Harbor

"Carolinians, you have been tested by fire, already. But now the time is at hand to show your mettle more than ever before!

"Let all able-bodied men rush to arms! Come fellow citizens; share with us our dangers, our brilliant success—or our glorious death!"

Published in various forms and distributed throughout the Carolinas, coastal Georgia, and parts of Tennessee, the proclamation issued about Thanksgiving 1862, was calculated to arouse everyone who read or heard it.

"That's Old Bory at his best," said admiring subordinates.

Pierre Gustave Toutant Beauregard was under no delusions. The hero of the assault upon Fort Sumter faced a much tougher fight this time; he would need all the manpower available.

In spite of the Federal blockade, tonnage of goods in and out of major Southern ports was near an all-time high. From Wilmington to Mobile—with Charleston and Savannah between—commerce with Britain and Europe flourished.

Nevertheless, intelligence reports from Confederate spies had assumed an alarming tone. Numerous ironclad ships were under construction by the U.S. Navy, and several were said to be ready to sail. The Confederates feared that the Federals would put everything into closing Southern ports. Beauregard, but not his superiors, believed that Charleston would be the target.

With the flagship at the rear, Du Pont's ironclads formed a line
across Charleston's harbor.

A flotilla of ironclads mounting guns larger than any
included in shore batteries, would mean a showdown.
The outcome of the conflict between sea power and con-
ventional land-based artillery could determine the course
of the war. It definitely would influence military strategy
for years to come.

Beauregard ordered more sandbags. Once Fort Moultrie
was as secure as he could make it, he turned his attention
to Castle Pinckney and Fort Sumter. Then he constructed
a line of signal stations arranged so that he could order
seventy-seven guns to fire simultaneously.

Torpedoes, the most effective mines then available,
were laid in the harbor. Nets made of huge hemp ropes

were arranged to hover just below the surface, ready to entangle propellers of vessels whose captains had out-of-date charts.

Waiting for the enemy to strike, men in Beauregard's command spent days in target practice. When marker buoys were hit, jubilant artillerymen carefully recorded wind conditions and distance.

Meanwhile Washington was as tense as Charleston, with spies under the leadership of Alan Pinkerton bringing back alarming news. At the rate Confederate preparations were being made, the Southern port would soon be invincible. Ironclads must strike soon, or not at all.

Admiral Samuel Du Pont, nephew of the pioneer munitions manufacturer, was selected to lead the assault against Charleston. He knew these waters, as he had scored the first decisive Union victory of the war at Port Royal. Even more important, he had reservations about the ability of ironclads to withstand heavy fire. That made him cautious; he was unwilling to mount an assault unless he was sure of winning.

At the U. S. Department of the Navy, top officials were openly jubilant. They believed once Du Pont had mastered Charleston, their invincible fleet would move south to Savannah. Then it would reduce Mobile before moving north to Wilmington to end Confederate capacity to engage in overseas trade.

To be sure that there would be no regrets, Assistant Secretary of the Navy Gustavus Fox persuaded superiors to give Du Pont the brand-new *Housatonic*. Rated at 1,200 tons, it was believed to be second only to the 3,500-ton flagship *New Ironsides* as the mightiest ship afloat.

Two gunboats, plus seven converted merchantmen, were to accompany the flagship. This was not so much because they would be needed, as the sight of a flotilla with thirty-three huge guns, plus many smaller ones, would throw panic into Confederate lookouts.

While the Federal plan sounded good, it didn't work out very well. Rebel artillerymen found an easy target in the ironclad *Keokuk*, conspicuous for her twin turrets.

When the warship ventured close to Fort Sumter, defenders scored ninety direct hits.

The size of the *New Ironsides* proved to be a liability rather than an asset. Inside the harbor the mighty ship moved clumsily. By darkness on the night of April 7, 1863, every ironclad in the Federal fleet was dented and scarred.

Scanning defensive works with glasses that night, Du Pont found little evidence of damage. "We'll resume the attack at dawn," he told his officers.

Daylight brought a quick revision in plans. Officers and men were hastily taken off the battered *Keokuk*. The only thing preventing it from sinking was that it had run aground on a sandbar. Damage to other ironclads was much worse than it had seemed at dusk; four would be unable to resume the assault under any circumstances.

Keenly aware that he would face censure or worse in Washington, Admiral Du Pont decided to accept defeat as the price of saving his men. Except for the *Keokuk*, the entire flotilla withdrew as rapidly as possible.

Immense naval guns had proved impotent, even when mounted on moving targets, when sent against skilled artillerymen who fired from protected fortifications. Not until World War I did a major power attempt another showdown such as that which took place in Charleston harbor on April 7, 1863.

General P. T. G. ("Ole Bory") Beauregard, Confederate commander.

30

The Battle That Changed Naval Warfare Forever

The most famous naval battle of the Civil War took place on March 16, 1862.

Union forces used the ironclad ship *Monitor*, designed and built with the goal of making wooden warships obsolete, while the Confederates had a converted wooden vessel which they had covered with a partial shield of iron. One-inch sheets of iron made in Atlanta and Richmond were applied in three layers to the partly burned Union gunboat *Merrimac*. Though the name *Merrimac* has stuck in many records, Confederates called their makeshift ironclad the CSS *Virginia*.

In order to fire, the *Virginia* had to turn because she carried just one seven-inch gun. There was no iron at points three or more feet below water. Worst of all, the *Virginia* could not maneuver in less than twenty-two feet of water.

Her rival, designed by famous inventor John Ericsson, had two eleven-inch guns inside a revolving turret. She was completely iron clad and had a draft of just twelve feet.

Most military experts would have said the clumsy *Virginia* didn't have a chance against the *Monitor*. Under the command of John L. Worden, the world's first warship designed and built as an ironclad left New York City.

Its destination was the Carolina coast, where it was to be stationed for blockade duty. But Confederates in the *Virginia* found the mighty ship in Hampton Roads, Virginia, and launched an attack.

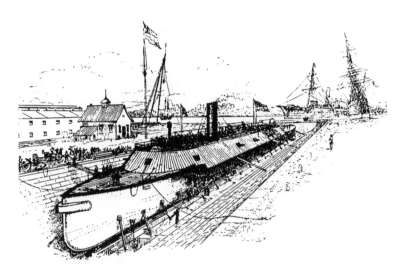

The Merrimac *under conversion into the* Virginia *at Norfolk.*

They fired at one another at close range for two hours. Both withdrew with no winner, but their meeting forever changed the navies of the world. Reporting the engagement, the *London Times* said there now were just two first class vessels in the world, both superior to Britain's 149 "first class warships."

Her enemies didn't know it, but the *Virginia* was crippled. Her smokestack was gone, and her steam pipes had been shot away. Railings, stanchions, and even boat davits had received direct hits. A rafter was cracked, and her engine, always creaky, failed frequently. Still, she had survived!

The jubilation of crew members was brief, for a series of Union victories drove Confederates from Norfolk and made capture of the *Virginia* seem inevitable.

Since Commodore Josiah Tattnall, head of the Confederate Navy, refused to allow the *Virginia* to fall into the hands of the enemy, he hastily scuttled the ship before it could be captured. To a court of inquiry, which exonerated him of wrongdoing, the crusty commodore tartly explained, "At least, we didn't lose a single man of our crew."

Union leaders decided to send the *Monitor* to Charleston, but she never reached her destination. On December 30, 1862, the ironclad hit heavy seas off Cape Hatteras and foundered. Four officers and twelve men perished with the vessel.

For more than one hundred years the *Monitor*'s whereabouts were unknown. A 1973 discovery showed her lying off the coast of North Carolina, bottom up, under 220 feet of water. Ambitious salvage schemes have been devised and promoted, but the vessel that inventor John Ericsson hailed as "totally invincible" remains a captive of the sea.

Eleven-inch guns of the Monitor.

INTERIOR OF   THE TOWER.

Neither the *Monitor* nor the *Virginia* (or *Merrimac*) ever won a victory of any consequence. But the four-hour battle of the two ironclads served notice that from that day on wooden warships—the standard for centuries—had become obsolete.

Sinking of the Monitor *off the Carolina coast.*

31

"Sherman in Gray" Burned a Wide Swath Around the World

"Put her to the torch, boys, and waste no time doing so!" ordered Capt. James Iredell Waddell. Master of the Confederate warship *Shenandoah*, North Carolina native Waddell had just captured his first prize, the Maine-owned bark *Alina*.

Headed toward Argentina, the unarmed merchant vessel posed no threat to fighting men in gray as her cargo consisted only of railroad iron. However, because she belonged to Yankees, destruction of the vessel would slightly weaken the Union cause.

Encountered in waters off Dakar in the Senegal, Africa, the cargo ship surrendered without a fight. She had no other choice; Waddell's vessel carried enough big guns to blow the *Alina* out of the water.

James D. Bullock of near Savannah had made a secret deal for the ship commanded by Waddell. In England, he bought the *Sea King*, with plans to outfit her as a warship. Soon after sailing from London on October 8, 1864, the ship was renamed the *Shenandoah* and took aboard heavy guns.

A smokestack, clearly visible in engravings of the era, reveals that although the ship was equipped with a full spread of sails, for some unaccountable reason it also had an auxilliary steam engine. Crew members of merchant vessels who noticed it were puzzled. James Waddell gloated. The engine gave him the extra speed he needed to overtake and capture Yankee ships.

Captain James I. Waddell of Pittsboro, Chatham County, North Carolina.

Having burned an unarmed merchant ship, the Confederate officer and his men had no place to hide. Under international law they had become pirates. Having nothing more to lose, they embarked on an eight-month voyage of destruction.

Gen. William Tecumseh Sherman, whom Henry Grady twitted as having been "a bit careless with fire," is hated for having burned Atlanta and destroyed Columbia, South Carolina. However, in terms of systematic, planned destruction, C.S.A. Capt. James Waddell was even more careless with fire on water than Sherman was on land.

After burning his first prize, Waddell captured and quickly disposed of three more vessels. By then his own ship was crowded with prisoners. Capture of the clipper ship *Kate Prince* offered a solution to overcrowding of the *Shenandoah*.

"I've taken four prizes, and I've burned four," Waddell told the master of the merchant vessel based in New Hampshire. "I'll spare yours if you'll take my prisoners to South America and sign a bond requiring your owners to pay $40,000 to the Confederate States of America."

Compared with the torch, those terms were lenient and generous. A bargain was struck, and the *Kate Prince* was soon on her way to Brazil.

Some of the many vessels burned by "North Carolina's Sherman in Gray" were: the *Lizzie Gray*, carrying barrel staves; the whale ship *Edward*; the whalers *Hector, Edward Carey, Pearl, Harvest, William Thompson,* and *Euphrates*.

Soon the Confederate seaman received troublesome news. One of the ships he had captured carried newspapers reporting the fall of Richmond, and the surrender of Robert E. Lee at Appomatox.

"Never mind," the Pittsboro, North Carolina, native told his crew members. "We're a long way from the action on the ground. We'll use the torch as long as we can."

Before the Confederate seaman was finished, he and his men burned at least thirty-one ships. Many were destroyed weeks after land forces of the Confederacy had ceased to fight.

A professional Navy man who enlisted as a midshipman in 1841, Waddell had studied at Annapolis and briefly taught there. He resigned his commission in January 1862 in order to become a lieutenant in the tiny Confederate navy.

As master of the *Shenandoah*, the Tar Heel was the only Confederate to carry the stars and bars around the world. He gave up the fight only when it became clear that the war had ended long ago on land. Finally he turned himself over to British authorities in November 1865.

When his vessel docked at Liverpool, it ended a voyage of 58,000 miles during which he had put into port only once, in Australia. Since he and his men were classified as pirates, they remained in England until President Andrew Johnson declared universal amnesty for former Confederates.

Waddell's global spree of capturing, pillaging, and burning puts him in a class by himself. No other man, whether wearing blue or gray, made such widespread use of fire as a form of punishment for enemy civilians.

Rare old photograph reveals sleek lines of the CSS Shenandoah.

PART SIX:

They Left Their Mark

Ann Pamela Cunningham. [Mount Vernon Ladies' Association]

32

Charleston Invalid Saved Mount Vernon for the Nation

Editors of the Charleston Mercury, widely regarded as the most influential newspaper in the South, did not balk at an open letter signed "A Southern Matron." After all, in 1853 it would have been unbecoming for a South Carolina lady to put her name in print, even at the end of an appeal addressed to "Ladies of the South." Not having the faintest idea of the writer's identity or place of residence, editors considered the letter worthy of use.

George Washington's ancestral home, said the missive, was falling into ruin. Members of the Washington family were unable to maintain it, and they had failed in attempts to have it purchased by the federal government or the state of Virginia.

Because of this melancholy situation, the estate would go to anyone who would pay the asking price, it was reliably reported. There was a good possibility that the site would be used for a resort hotel.

This need not, should not, and must not happen, said the letter writer. Ladies of the South could and surely would, by joint efforts "in village and country square and city" secure "from the mites of thousands of gentle hearts" the money needed to save Mount Vernon.

Years later it was found that "A Southern Matron" was unmarried and was really Ann Pamela Cunningham. Member of a distinguished Laurens County family, she had been crippled in girlhood by a fall from a horse. Yet the semi-invalid who preferred to remain anonymous had the courage also to send a proposal to John A. Washington, Jr. Ladies of the South, she said, would like to purchase Mount Vernon, the sooner the better.

Washington, who had let it be known he'd consider nothing under $200,000 did not bother to acknowledge receipt of the letter from South Carolina.

In Mobile, editors of the *Herald and Tribune* saw and reprinted the plea from the Charleston *Mercury*. Like it or not, the nation was going to be exposed to an idealistic woman's dream.

At a little church near Rosemonte, the Cunningham home, ladies met early in 1854 to form the Mount Vernon Ladies' Association. Ann Pamela's mother, who presided, headed the subscription list, donating one hundred dollars.

Other meetings were held in Laurens, South Carolina, and in Savannah. They yielded several hundred more dollars.

Mrs. Philoclea Eve, of Augusta, Georgia, a "cousin by marriage" of Ann Pamela, published a letter of her own. It deplored America's forgetting Washington and asked for help.

A fellow Augusta resident, Mrs. Tubman, responded with three hundred dollars, one hundred dollars each "for the state where I was born, the state where I was married, and the state where I now live."

Before Augusta ladies stopped voicing pleas, residents gave more than three thousand dollars—twenty-five cents each for every man, woman, and child in the city.

In Mobile and Richmond, ladies joined the effort. Responding to a plaintive plea from Philadelphia, leaders of the still anonymously led movement graciously agreed to permit ladies of the North to join the movement to save the shrine.

Even so, it seemed ludicrous to ordinary folk that a group of women thought they could raise two hundred thousand dollars. However, Edward Everett of Boston did not share that view. Renowned as one of the nation's most sought-after orators, he volunteered to speak on behalf of the ladies and their dream.

Everett prepared a special Washington address, then delivered it 129 times. Traveling always at his own expense, he added fifty-five thousand dollars to the cause. Soon the Mount Vernon Ladies' Association was in a position to buy the property.

Nevertheless, before they could purchase it, they would need to have something no other ladies' group had ever gained, a charter. Once the Virginia legislature acted upon their request, they bought the entire Mount Vernon site of approximately five hundred acres.

To this day the Mount Vernon Ladies' Association operates what has become one of America's most loved shrines. Enlarged and expanded through the years to include outbuildings and gardens designed by Washington, their holdings are now being completely refurbished as a result of another successful financial campaign, this time for ten million dollars.

Open to visitors every day of the year, Mount Vernon sits on a bluff two hundred feet above the Potomac River at a point where it is nearly two miles wide. Few visitors realize that the breathtaking estate would not be there without the work of idealistic, determined Carolina women.

33

Dolley Madison Was One Step Ahead of the British

James Madison had given precise instructions. If there were any signs that the British might enter Washington, his wife was to flee instantly. She should take along as many official papers as possible and meet him at Wiley's Tavern on the south bank of the Potomac River.

Then age 63, the president became our nation's first and only sitting chief executive to go into battle. He was unwilling for others to risk their lives if he did not, so he led a small band of fighting men in the futile effort to turn back the British.

August 24, 1814, brought ominous portents. Sounds that ordinarily would have been dismissed as distant thunder were quickly identified as the firing of British cannons. Soon soldiers were seen running through the streets.

"Our enemies have entered the city!" a messenger informed Dolley Madison. "Their advance guard is only minutes away!"

Many official documents had already been packed in trunks. Servants began loading them in carriages, while their mistress turned her attention to the executive mansion itself. Completed only a few years earlier, the residence of the president was still sparsely furnished.

Clearly, though, one item was beyond replacement. A splendid portrait of George Washington, skillfully framed, was an object of universal admiration.

Dolley stood by as an aide attempted to rip the frame from the wall, but it refused to budge. Reacting instinctively, the mistress of the White House seized a long kitchen knife and cut the prized painting from its frame.

Rolling up the Washington portrait, Mrs. Madison fled as fast as the horses would take her. She was barely out of sight before redcoats entered the vacated mansion. They looted it of everything considered valuable, then set fire to it. By the time the flames died down, only the outer walls were relatively undamaged.

James Madison, who accomplished little or nothing in his role of commander-in-chief in the field, was watching from a distance when much of the nation's capital went up in flames. He dashed about on horseback for two days, but failed to reach Wiley's Tavern.

Both the president and his wife returned to the charred ruins of Washington City on August 27, after the British withdrew to move toward coastal targets. They were forced to seek temporary quarters in the "Octagon House" because their residence was unusable.

Dolley Madison never again entered the executive mansion as its mistress. Restoration took more than two years,

*Dolley Madison,
Carolina-born queen
of Washington society.*
[NATIONAL ARCHIVES]

and by then James Monroe was president. Completely re-furbished and painted white to conceal telltale signs of damage, the residence became popularly known as the White House.

Today the White House has only one article of furnish-ing from the original executive mansion: the splendid portrait of George Washington. Had it not been for quick action by Dolley Madison, the portrait would have gone up in flames.

The woman who saved that portrait was a Tar Heel by birth. Her Virginia parents came to the Quaker settlement of New Garden, North Carolina, to spend a year with a relative. There a child believed to have been their third—and their first daughter—was born in 1768.

Guilford County lore insists that the little girl was named Dorothea Dandridge, in honor of Patrick Henry's second wife. She became Dolley in the family circle and entered history under that name.

Long before becoming mistress of the executive man-sion, Dolley had served as hostess for Thomas Jefferson. After the death of her own husband, she returned to Washington and reigned as queen of society in the na-tion's capital for years.

"In length and popular acclaim," declares the au-thoritative *Dictionary of American Biography*, the Car-olina woman remembered for having been one step ahead of the British, reigned over official society in a fashion that "has had no parallel in American history."

Only the charred shell of the executive mansion remained when the British left.

34

Calhoun Sowed Seeds That Led to War

"We hold it as unquestionable that on the separation from the Crown of Great Britain, the people of the several colonies became free and independent states," said John C. Calhoun in an "Address to the People of the United States" in 1832.

Although few Americans, in the North or the South, disagreed with that verdict, the introductory statement hardly prepared readers for what followed: "We hold it equally unquestionable that the Constitution of the United States is a compact between the people of the several states, constituting free, independent, and sovereign communities."

Especially, but not exclusively, in Washington, such an idea bordered upon treason. If the states making up the nation were free and independent, they would do as they pleased about edicts of the national government.

That is precisely what South Carolina had done, at the urging of the state's most persuasive political spokesman. Furious that the tariff of 1828 discriminated against the South, Vice President John C. Calhoun had resigned. He preferred to devote his time to the U.S. Senate, he said, where he could continue to fight the bill.

Even Calhoun was unable to persuade a majority of senators to come to the aid of the South, which he said had been "pillaged, even raped, by Federal legislation."

For at least four years, probably longer, Calhoun had been brooding about the growing tension between federal and state authority. He drafted a long paper entitled

139

"South Carolina Exposition" but did not release it. Even Calhoun realized that publication could lead to a national crisis. But when South Carolina passed an Ordinance of Nullification on November 24, 1832, Calhoun drew upon this paper when he set out to convince the nation of the correctness of the action.

Under its terms, Congressional tariff acts were declared null and void within the Palmetto State. Collection of duties was forbidden, and every officeholder in the state was required to take an oath supporting the Nullification Act.

Finally—and perhaps most important—Carolinians pledged themselves, through elected leaders who framed the ordinance, to denounce any and all efforts of the national government to enforce the tariff. If strong measures of enforcement were tried, South Carolina warned, the state would immediately proceed to organize a separate government.

There had been talk of withdrawal from the Union much earlier, mostly in the northeast. Proponents pointed out that the Constitution did not prohibit such action by individual states.

Decades had passed, however, and the Union had held firm. Ordinary citizens had come to feel that state authority took second place to federal authority.

While never actually attempted, the notion of secession was nearly as old as the nation, but nullification was an entirely different matter. Under Calhoun's doctrine a state could—and in the case of South Carolina already had—formally declare acts of Congress to be null and void.

Andrew Jackson, widely claimed as a native son of South Carolina, was in the White House. He had given his personal support to the tariff acts. If his own state were to thumb its nose at Washington, the entire national structure could crumble.

"They can talk and write resolutions and print threats to their hearts' content," thundered Old Hickory. "If one drop of blood is shed in defiance of the laws of the United States, I will hang the first man of them I can get my hands on, to the first tree I can find."

During the spring of 1833, that threat by Jackson was pondered and debated throughout the nation. In the South many town meetings saw resolutions of defiance greeted by shouts of approval. Old cartoons depicting Jackson as a hangman and as King Andrew I were reprinted and widely distributed, and Jackson responded by setting in motion the machinery needed to send federal troops into South Carolina to enforce federal laws.

Henry Clay, who frankly admitted that Pennsylvania, Massachusetts, New York, and New Jersey were growing rich at the expense of the Carolinas, Georgia, Alabama, and Tennessee, framed what he called "a compromise tariff."

Somewhat mollified by the small concessions gained under the compromise and keenly aware that federal troops were being assembled for invasion, South Carolina retreated. Legislators repealed the ordinance of nullification, and the collection of the hated tariff was resumed in the state.

The union was intact, for the moment. But when the concept of nullification was added to the injustice of economic discrimination and the evils of slavery, civil war became inevitable. It was no longer a question of whether it would come, but when and under what circumstances.

Yet it is doubtful that in 1833 even fiery John C. Calhoun would have predicted that the first shots of the Civil War would be fired in Charleston, where he is buried. Had the old war horse sensed it, he would have been delighted.

35

Runaway Apprentice Beats the Impeachment Process

"Ran away from the Subscriber two apprentice boys, legally bound, named William and Andrew. I will pay ten dollars to any person who will deliver the said apprentices to me in Raleigh, or I will give the above Reward for Andrew Johnson alone."

James J. Selby's advertisement in North Carolina's *Raleigh Gazette* of June 24, 1824, points to a now-forgotten form of bondage. Indentured servants, or "white slaves," played crucial roles in European colonization of our continent and in later U.S. history.

British lawyers and political leaders invented the device in response to a problem.

Initially hundreds, then thousands, of persons who wanted to go to the New World had no money for passage. Recognizing the opportunity to profit, wealthy British leaders devised indentured servitude, an arrangement by which people could swap years of labor for the price of an ocean voyage.

Once launched, the practice of using a labor contract in lieu of cash mushroomed. Ships' owners and masters offered to take desperate persons to Virginia, Carolina, or other colonies once the proper papers were signed.

Usually, but not always, the term of service was seven years. An indentured servant was given a room, food, and clothing, but no cash.

In contrast, black slaves were bought and sold like any other merchandise. As the system of "white slavery" became more deeply entrenched, it offered other opportunities to brokers who bought and sold papers of indenture.

Some desperate parents signed papers by which, in exchange for a small amount of cash, they bound out their sons and daughters. Orphans and youthful paupers, who were wards of the community, were commonly placed in work houses or were forced into seven years of servitude under papers of indenture.

Refugee servant Andrew Johnson, age fifteen, was not recovered by his master. Walking about seventy-five miles to the southwest, he found refuge in Carthage, North Carolina. There the trade he was learning as a servant to Selby, a prosperous tailor, proved to be his salvation.

Johnson worked as a tailor in Carthage, then proceeded to Laurens, South Carolina. From there he made a secret trip to Raleigh.

Andrew Johnson's tailor shop in Greeneville, Tennessee.
[North Carolina Department of Archives and History]

President Andrew Johnson.

Still legally a fugitive, the boy persuaded his mother (who had bound him out) that he was now able to earn a living for them. Accompanied by her second husband, a weaver and spinner, Mary Johnson Dougherty went west with her son. They traveled in a one-horse cart carrying all their belongings.

Reaching Greeneville, Tennessee, they discovered that

the town tailor was ready to retire. So at age seventeen the former indentured servant hung out his shingle and went into business as "A. Johnson, Tailor."

Though he had never spent a day in school, Johnson learned to read and to write. He pored over books, especially those containing the speeches of great English orators. Fellow townsmen admired their self-taught tailor so much they made him an alderman. Then he was elected mayor of Greeneville.

Moving up the political ladder step by step, Johnson was successively a member of the Tennessee house of representatives, a Tennessee state senator, and a member of the U. S. House of Representatives. He then became governor of Tennessee and a member of the U. S. Senate.

It was while serving as senator that he was hand-picked by federal authorities in 1862 to become military governor of Tennessee. His outspoken loyalty to the Union brought him the vice presidency, and the assassination of Lincoln put him in the White House.

There the man who had laid his life on the line for the Union was subjected to attack for his "pro-Southern views." A struggle with Congress, centering on Johnson's desire to do all he could to heal the wounds of the Civil War, led to the first and only impeachment trial of a chief executive.

The man who had fled from Raleigh as a boy asked for forty days to prepare his defense; foes gave him only ten. Eleven articles of impeachment spelled out his "high crimes and misdemeanors."

With fifty-four Senators sitting as judges, President Johnson would have been found guilty if two-thirds of the body had voted against him. A crucial vote saw thirty-five senators concurring that he was, indeed, guilty as charged. That total was just one vote short of the crucial two-thirds required.

John F. Kennedy's *Profiles in Courage* deals in depth with the Republican senator, Edmund G. Ross of Kansas, whose support of Andrew Johnson saved him from conviction.

Ticket of admission to impeachment proceedings. [NATIONAL ARCHIVES]

One other U.S. president, Millard Fillmore, was an indentured servant. At age fourteen he was apprenticed by his father to a clothmaker.

But ex-apprentice Andrew Johnson of Raleigh is in a class all by himself. He is the only chief executive to have faced formal impeachment proceedings, and won, in spite of being an unwilling player in a game in which the deck was stacked.

36
Joel Poinsett's "Ghost" Is Here Every Christmas

Writing from Philadelphia on December 1, 1835, florist R. Buist bubbled with enthusiasm. "In our collection last winter," he wrote, "the beautiful scarlet bractii on a Mexican imported plant four months from cutting reached fourteen inches in diameter."

Buist had earlier notified Charleston-born Joel R. Poinsett that the exciting new plant would be called the poinsettia in his honor.

The plant had created excitement among botanists at the Royal Botanic Garden in Edinburgh, Scotland, soon after having been brought from Mexico by Poinsett in 1828. Yet no one on either side of the Atlantic then anticipated what would take place. It has become *the* modern Christmas flower.

Nearly forgotten today, Joel Poinsett was in his era the most urbane American to hold high national office.

British redcoats occupied Charles Town at the time of his birth in 1779. Therefore his prosperous father, a Huguenot physician, packed up the family when Joel was three and took them to England for six years. That could have fostered what proved to be a life-long absorption with foreign travel.

After studying medicine for a year, Poinsett set aside his books to spend several months in Scotland and in Portugal. He then spent a year in France, followed by leisurely travel through Switzerland, Germany, and Italy. Then he came home to spend two years touring North

Joel R. Poinsett.
[Nineteenth century engraving]

America by horseback and boat. Soon he left on an ex-
tended trip to Russia and her Asian frontiers.

A few months after returning to the United States in
1810, the world traveler was sent to Chile as the first official North American emissary to Spanish-speaking
South America. After playing a key role in Chile's fight for
independence, he returned to South Carolina and served
two terms in Congress.

Following his inauguration President John Quincy
Adams chose Poinsett as the United States' first minister
to Mexico. Ironically, Poinsett had spent more years outside our nation than in it.

December 1825, was an exciting time for avid botanist
Joel Poinsett. In every marketplace, he found Mexicans
offering a colorful flower for sale. They called it "The
Flower of the Holy Night" because it was at the height of
its brilliance on December 25.

Poinsett examined the plant and discovered that the bright red displays are not blossoms. Instead, he found them to be bracts, or petal-like leaves; the true flower of the plant is the tiny but vivid yellow cluster at its center.

The end of Poinsett's tour of duty in Mexico began with the elections of 1828, which set off a revolt. Having sided with the insurgents, Poinsett found himself in the middle of the action.

"In Mexico City, the house of the American ambassador was the refuge of the persecuted," he later recalled. "It was pointed out to the infuriated military, and they rushed to the attack.

"My only defense was the flag of my country. It was flung out at the instant that hundreds of muskets were leveled at the embassy."

Poinsett's friends and allies prevailed, but so many Mexicans resented his having meddled in their affairs that Andrew Jackson recalled him. Forced to leave Mexico City on Christmas Day 1829, he took with him cuttings of the wildflower that to Mexicans was simply a weed, except at Christmas.

Four years' service as U.S. secretary of war in an era of tension (1837–41) is Poinsett's chief claim to national fame. During this period, he upgraded the U.S. Military Academy at West Point to an unprecedented level of importance in our nation's defense. Yet his most enduring legacy is the "Mexican weed" he introduced to the United States and Europe.

Early fanciers were puzzled. Growing wild in Mexico, plants turned many a hillside red as Christmas approached. But in Philadelphia and London they remained green during December.

Years of experiment showed that the intensity and duration of light governs the growth cycle of the plant. Commercial growers have learned to control exposure to light. Hence, millions of plants bearing the name of Joel Poinsett are now at their peak beauty precisely at Christmas in most major cities of the world.

37

Charlestonian Added Twenty-Eight Million Acres to the Nation

"Mr. President, we must ignore critics," said U. S. Secretary of War Jefferson Davis. "History will judge us by what we do about the Mesilla Valley. I urge that we send new instructions to Gadsden."

Already committed to the goal of securing a land grant from Mexico, President Franklin Pierce mused briefly. In his imagination he could see a transcontinental railroad snaking its way through the region south of Arizona's Gila River.

"Send for Marcy," he directed. "Final arrangements belong to him and his department."

U.S. Secretary of State William L. Marcy, weak and indecisive, had abolitionist sentiments. That meant he leaned toward a northern route for the contemplated rail line.

A southern route, considered least expensive of three under consideration, would bring new industry to the entire South. A rush of settlers would help maintain the delicate balance between pro- and antislavery states. Davis was determined to get the coveted land.

As a key actor in the international drama, Jefferson Davis's friend James Gadsden would have to conduct the negotiations. A native of Charleston, Gadsden had piled up an impressive track record by the time Franklin Pierce took office in 1853.

Gadsden had gone into Florida with Andrew Jackson as his adjutant general during the Seminole War and had remained in the conquered region to supervise the removal

James Gadsden. [Gibbs Art Gallery]

of the Seminole Indians to reservations and to build Florida's first roads.

Back home by 1840, he became president of the Louisville, Cincinnati, & Charleston Railroad. If he was not the first man of influence to advocate creation of a strong southern rail network, he was perhaps the most persuasive early spokesman for this cause.

At Memphis in 1845, Gadsden caused delegates to a regional commercial convention to take better notice of tiny Atlanta. Small as it was, he insisted, it was a vital rail center sure to gain rapidly in importance.

It was at this convention that the Charlestonian suggested building a transcontinental railroad "along an easy and economical southern route." To make that possible, the United States would have to acquire thousands of square miles from Mexico.

Stressing Gadsden's "extraordinary vision" and experience as a rail executive, Jefferson Davis helped win him a hearing. Franklin Pierce was so impressed that in 1853 he named the South Carolinian as minister to Mexico.

Gadsden had been in Mexico City only a few weeks before he sent an optimistic report. "Times are very hard here," he wrote. "Money is so scarce that some of the governmental departments seldom meet their payrolls on time. An offer of hard cash, right now, can hardly be refused. Perhaps we can get even more land than we actually need for the railroad."

This intriguing report led Jefferson Davis to push for immediate action. Fearful of Mexican bandits, Davis persuaded the secretary of state to take unprecedented action.

Once Gadsden's new instructions had been prepared, they were delivered to Christopher L. Ward as messenger. In order to foil bandits, Ward was required to memorize long and detailed orders so, if captured, he would have no documents on his person.

There's no certainty that Ward remembered every detail committed to him. What he did recall, he relayed to Gadsden in Mexico City.

This chain of events had the effect of giving the Charlestonian a free hand. Having no written instructions, he could proceed as he wished, then claim that Ward forgot or misunderstood debatable points.

Gadsden immediately went into a series of negotiations, emerging with a treaty he had drafted. For ten million dollars, the United States was to get more than twenty-eight million acres in the vital Mesilla Valley. Ratified in 1854, the treaty established the present boundary between Mexico and the United States.

In 1869 the United States became the first continent to have a rail line from coast to coast, when the Union Pacific and Central Pacific lines met at Promontory, Utah. Gadsden's dream became a reality when the Southern Pacific Railroad was completed in 1882.

Small by comparison with the Louisiana and Alaska purchases, the Gadsden Purchase was immensely profitable; it brought our nation a region estimated to have yielded ten billion dollars in minerals alone. Within one hundred years the annual payroll of the Southern Pacific Railroad topped the purchase price.

One crucial aspect is nearly forgotten now. James Gadsden, Jefferson Davis, and Franklin Pierce knew that money paid by the United States would not go into the sagging Mexican economy.

Money for the Gadsden Purchase went directly into the pockets of dictator Santa Anna, the universally hated military dictator responsible for the massacre of Americans at the Alamo.

38

Charles Frémont Was First To Free the Slaves

Few instructors paid much attention to Charles Frémont at the College of Charleston. In that blue-blooded city, his illegitimate birth was a stain that, most natives agreed, no achievement could ever erase.

That verdict seemed to be confirmed in 1831 when he was expelled from the college for irregular attendance. At least, that's what the record said. It was whispered that Frémont "had abolitionist leanings." Even the rumor would have been enough to cause school authorities to get rid of him.

After a hitch on the U.S. sloop of war *Natchez*, the man born in Savannah, Georgia (but largely reared in Charleston) returned to the Palmetto State. There he won a spot in a special detail whose duty it was to map the Cherokee lands of North Carolina, Tennessee, and Georgia.

By 1841 the man who had not finished college had won as his bride the beautiful Jessie Benton, daughter of a powerful U.S. senator. It was as her husband that he proposed to lead an expedition to explore and map the Rocky Mountains. Backed by his father-in-law, he won the post.

Charles Frémont became an explorer whose lasting contributions were perhaps a bit below those of Lewis and Clark, but they were significant and permanent. From the mountains, he turned to California.

There he helped to organize "the Bear Flag Republic" and gained control of its military organization. From that post, he became civil governor of California, by then recognized as a U.S. territory. California sent him to Washington as a senator, and in 1856 he was the first Republican candidate for the presidency.

Small wonder that Frémont was eyed with caution by many national leaders. He was too threatening for anyone with ambition to take him casually.

It was as a major general of volunteers that he marched into Missouri at the outbreak of the Civil War. He was the military head of the entire region from the Mississippi River to the Rocky Mountains.

Lincoln himself frequently conferred with Frémont, once commiserating with his field commander over the fact that 8,000 of his 23,000 men were "three-month soldiers." In the early days of the war, the president had discovered that men who had enlisted for only ninety days were worse than useless for long-term campaigns. They'd be back on the farm or in factories before the first shot could be fired. Worse, they consumed food and used clothing that could be put to better use.

When Frémont reached St. Louis, he telegraphed his commander-in-chief that he had "absolutely no arms." In this emergency "the little bastard from Carolina" sent a squad of his men to the U.S. paymaster with orders to bring back $100,000, by force, if necessary.

With the money seized without authorization, Frémont equipped his men for a series of lightning-like raids. It took little more than a month to seize firm control of the vital border state.

From St. Louis on August 31, 1861, John Charles Frémont issued a proclamation establishing martial law throughout Missouri and ordering the seizure of property belonging to "persons in rebellion against the United States." As if these stern measures were not enough, Frémont's edict also declared that slaves belonging to rebels were declared free. The last clause set Washington into an uproar.

Emancipation had been discussed often and at length, partly at the insistence of Secretary of State William H.

Seward. Each time, conferees flatly rejected the notion for the foreseeable future. Maybe some time, they agreed, but not now.

Abraham Lincoln fired off a furious message to the head of the Western Department. In it, he requested Frémont to withdraw his proclamation of emancipation.

Frémont refused. As commander-in-chief, the president made it clear that he expected to be obeyed or else.

The president, who was not ready to sanction the freeing of slaves in a border state in 1861, never forgave Frémont for having jumped the gun. He sent investigators into Missouri, where they found evidence that permitted Washington to remove the abolitionist from command.

Even standard reference works often fail to mention Frémont's abolition of Missouri slaves. If he were alive, he would not care. Always a champion of the underdog (perhaps as a result of brooding over his illegitimate birth), he had a consuming goal of aiding persons whom society exploited.

Sixteen months later, at a time he considered politically expedient, Abraham Lincoln issued his own Emancipation Proclamation. More than any other presidential order, it made him world famous as "the great emancipator."

That Lincoln received the glory for emancipation meant little to Frémont. But he never forgave him that most Missouri slaves spent an unnecessary sixteen months in bondage.

Index

157

Boldface signifies an illustration.